CONTENTS

D0402035

A WORD OF ADVICE

If you are planning a trip to Japan, you will find that your enjoyment of your stay there will be increased many times if you speak Japanese with the people you encounter. Nothing will ease your travels more dramatically than the willingness (*and* ability) to express yourself to the people you will encounter in their own language.

Do not be afraid to use these words, pronouncing them according to the phonetic key which follows each word and sentence in this book. By practicing a little and listening to the inhabitants of the country, you will soon be using Japanese with correct native accent and inflection. Don't let your friends tell you that you can get along by speaking only English! Remember, a native of Japan could "get along" in Pittsburgh by speaking only Japanese, in that, if he used sign language astutely, he probably would not starve to death. But would this hypothetical Japanese in his travels in America make any friends, have any enjoyable experiences, or take home any memories of the country that he could not get from picture postcards?

From the minute you set foot in Japan you will find that the use of the prepared phrases in this book will not only facilitate your travels and help you in emergencies, but will make your everyday contacts a thousand times more effective, save you money, and make your trip a fascinating adventure.

HOW TO PRONOUNCE IT

Although Japanese is usually written in a combination of written characters or ideographs and a flowing syllable alphabet called Hiragana, it is also possible to write it in the Roman letters we use which the Japanese call Roma-Ji. In order to make your pronunciation difficulties practically non-existent, we have devised a simple phonetic rendition of each Japanese word which appears in italics underneath it. Pronounce this just the way it looks and the average Japanese will have no difficulty in understanding you. Take the word "kimono" for instance. Pronounce it *kee-moh-noh,* pronouncing each syllable with more or less equal emphasis. Simple, isn't it? Nothing can take the place of the accent of a native, however, so keep your ears open and try to copy the accent of the Japanese you meet. You will be interested to note that there is no "l" sound in Japanese pronunciation; it just doesn't exist. There are practically no other pitfalls in Japanese pronunciation, except that the letter "u" is sometimes pronounced and sometimes skipped over. We have indicated this in our phonetic rendition.

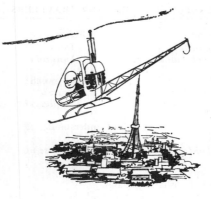

I

BEFORE YOU LAND IN JAPAN

In this book you will find words and phrases for almost any immediate situation that you may encounter during your visit to Japan. However, before you land we recommend that you learn by heart the following basic vocabulary which you will find useful every time you speak to a Japanese.

Yes.	**No.**	**Thank you.**
Hai.	Iie.	Arigatō.
High.	*Ee-yeh.*	*Ah-ree-gah-*TOH.

You are welcome.
Dō itashimashite.
DOH *ee-tah-shee-mah-shee-teh.*

1

Excuse me.
  Gomennasai.
  Goh-meh-nah-sah'ee.

Please.
  Dōzo.
  Doh-*zoh.*

All right.
  Yoroshii desu.
  Yoh-roh-shee'ee dehss.

How much?
  Ikura?
  Ee-koo-rah?

Where?
  Doko?
  Doh-koh?

I do not understand.
  Wakarimasen.
  Wah-kah-ree-mah-sehn.

Please repeat.
  Mo ichido oshatte kudasai.
  Moh ee-chee-doh oh-shaht-teh koo-dah-sah'ee.

Good morning.
  Ohayō.
  *Oh-high-*YOH.

Good day (or) **Good afternoon.**
  Konnichiwa.
  Kohn-nee-chee-wah.

Good evening.
  Konbanwa.
  Kohn-bahn-wah.

Good-by.
  Sayōnara.
  *Sah-*YOH-*nah-rah.*

Delighted to meet you.
  Dōzo yorishiku.
  Doh-*zoh yoh-ree-shee-koo.*

How are you?
  Ikaga desu ka?
  Ee-kah-gah dehss kah?

Very well, thank you, and you?
  Okagesama de genki desu. Anata wa?
  Oh-kah-gheh-sah-mah deh ghehn-kee dehss. Ah-nah-tah wah?

WATCH THAT ACCENT

Although Japanese is generally quite easy to pronounce, the "u," as you have noticed in the words above, is sometimes not sounded. For example, the word "desu," meaning "is" or "are," is written as *dehss* in the phonetics.

Also note that, except in rare cases, the syllables in Japanese words have more or less equal stress. In the rare cases when they don't, we have printed the stressed syllable in the phonetics in small capitals, as in the case of "dozo" (DOH-*zoh*) the word for "please."

Before you land, it is also a good idea to learn the numbers from 1 to 10. Here they are:

1	2	3	4	5
ichi	ni	san	shi (yon)	go
ee-chee	*nee*	*sahn*	*shee (yohn)*	*goh*

6	7	8	9	10
roku	shichi	hachi	ku	jū
roh-koo	*shee-chee*	*hah-chee*	*koo*	JOO

AN INTERESTING NOTE

The word "shi" (four) may be rendered as "yon" because "shi" also means "death" and the courteous Japanese often uses this substitute to avoid the depressing similarity

II

WHEN YOU ARRIVE IN JAPAN

You will find the following expressions extremely useful at any port of entry. Remember, any Japanese will immediately adopt a more friendly attitude toward you if you make an attempt to speak even a few words of his language. It is flattering to the people to whom you speak and shows that you are interested in Japan.

Here is my passport.
Watakushi no ryoken desu.
Wah-tahk-shee noh r'yoh-kehn dehss.

May I go through?
Tōtte mo yoroshii desu ka?
Toht-teh moh yoh-roh-shee'ee dehss kah?

4

That is my bag.
Are wa watakushi no kaban desu.
Ah-reh wah wah-tahk-shee noh kah-bahn dehss.

Here, please.
Koko ni dōzo.
Koh-koh nee DOH-*zoh.*

Over there.
Achira ni.
Ah-chee-rah nee.

Here are my checks.
Watakushi no hikikaeken desu.
Wah-tahk-shee noh hee-kee-kah-eh-kehn dehss.

I have nothing to declare.
Watakushi wa betsu ni shinkoku suru koto wa
arimasen.
Wah-tahk-shee wah beht-soo nee sheen-koh-koo
soo-roo koh-toh wah ah-ree-mah-sehn.

Is it all right to close them?
Shimete mo yoroshii desu ka?
Shee-meh-teh moh yoh-roh-shee'ee dehss kah?

Take them to a taxi, please.
Takushī ni annai shite kudasai.
*Tahk-*SHEE *nee ahn-nah'ee shee-teh koo-dah-sah'ee.*

Bring them here, please.
Dōzo kochira ni omochi kudasai.
DOH-*zoh koh-chee-rah nee oh-moh-chee koo-dah-*
sah'ee.

Where is the men's room?
Otoko no benjo wa doko desu ka?
Oh-toh-koh noh behn-joh wah doh-koh dehss kah?

Where is the ladies' room?
Onna no gofujo wa doko desu ka?
Ohn-nah noh goh-foo-joh wah doh-koh dehss kah?

Take me to the Hotel Okura.
Ōkura hoteru made itte kudasai.
Oн-*koo-rah hoh-teh-roo mah-deh eet-teh koo-dah-sah'ee.*

Where can I change money?
Doko de okane wo kaeru koto ga dekimasu ka?
Doh-koh deh oh-kah-neh woh kah-eh-roo koh-toh gah deh-kee-mahss kah?

What is the rate for the dollar?
Doru no kawase sōba wa ikura deshō ka?
Doh-roo noh kah-wah-seh soн-*bah wah ee-koo-rah deh-*sнoн *kah?*

Please change this money into yen.
Yen ni kaete kudasai.
Yehn nee kah-eh-teh koo-dah-sah'ee.

Now, since a dollar is worth several hundred
yen, you had better learn some bigger numbers.
Here they are up to 100:

11	12	13
jūichi	jūni	jūsan
ɟoo-*ee-chee*	ɟoo-*nee*	ɟoo-*sahn*

14	15	16
jūshi	jūgo	jūroku
ɟoo-*shee*	ɟoo-*goh*	ɟoo-*roh-koo*

17	18	19
jūshichi	jūhachi	jūku
JOO-*shee-chee*	JOO-*hah-chee*	JOO-*koo*

20	21	22
nijū	nijūichi	nijūni
nee-JOO	*nee*-JOO-*ee-chee*	*nee*-JOO-*nee*

28	30
nijūhachi	sanjū
nee-JOO-*hah-chee*	*sahn*-JOO

40		50
yonjū (or) shijū		gojū
yohn-JOO *shee*-JOO		*goh*-JOO

60	70
rokujū	hichijū
roh-koo-JOO	*hee-chee*-JOO

80	90	100
hachijū	kyujū	hyaku
hah-chee-JOO	*k'yoo*-JOO	*h'yah-koo*

Here are some things that people are likely to say to you, and some short answers you may use.

Your name?	**Nationality?**
O namae wa?	Kokuseki wa?
Oh nah-mah-eh wah?	*Koh-koo-seh-kee wah?*

American.	**British.**
America-jin.	Ei-koku-jin.
Ah-meh-ree-kah-jin.	*Eh-koh-koo-jin.*

Canadian.	**Japanese.**
Kanada-jin.	Nihon-jin.
Kah-nah-dah-jin.	*Nee-hohn-jin.*

Address in Tokyo?
Tōkyō no jūsho wa?
Тон-k'yoh noh joo-shoh wah?

Hotel Okura.
Ōkura hoteru.
Oн-koo-rah hoh-teh-roo.

Health certificate?
Kenkō shindansho?
Kehn-кoн sheen-dahn-shoh?

Here you are!
Hai dōzo!
High DOH-zoh!

How much do you wish to change?
Ikura kaemasu ka?
Ee-koo-rah kah'eh-mahss kah?

$75.
Nanajūgo doru.
Nah-nah-joo-goh doh-roo.

Where are your bags?
Anata no kaban wa doko desu ka?
*Ah-nah-tah noh kah-bahn wah doh-koh dehss
kah?*

Over there.
Achira desu.
Ah-chee-rah dehss.

Have you anything to declare?
Betsu ni shinkoku suru koto wa arimasen ka?
*Beht-soo nee sheen-koh-koo soo-roo koh-toh wah
ah-ree-mah-sehn kah?*

Nothing.   **Is that all?**
  Arimasen.   Kore dake desu ka?
  Ah-ree-mah-sehn. *Koh-reh dah-keh dehss kah?*

Yes, that's all.
  Hai, kore dake desu.
  High, koh-reh dah-keh dehss.

Where do you wish to go?
  Dochira ni ikaremasu ka?
  Doh-chee-rah nee ee-kah-reh-mahss kah?

To the Imperial Hotel.
  Teikoku hoteru ni ikimasu.
  Teh'ee-koh-koo hoh-teh-roo nee ee-kee-mahss.

Are you alone?
  O hitori sama desu ka?
  Oh hee-toh-ree sah-mah dehss kah?

Are you together?
  Go isho desu ka?
  Goh ee-shoh dehss kah?

NOTE: Japanese are very polite. Besides the custom of bowing when greeting and leaving people (and, frequently, in between), the suffix "san" meaning honorable is attached to the names or titles of people whom you are addressing. If you have a friend named Yamada, for instance, you call him Yamada-san. And in speaking to a hotel bellboy you address him as "boi-san" and a waitress as "kyūji-san," literally "honorable waitress."

III

AT YOUR HOTEL

Usually you will find that hotel desk clerks in large cities speak English. But by all means use Japanese with the rest of the hotel staff.

Where is a good hotel?

Shinyō no aru hoteru wa doko desu ka?

Shee-n'YOH noh ah-roo hoh-teh-roo wah doh-koh dehss kah?

Are the prices reasonable?

Onedan wa tegoro desu ka?

Oh-neh-dahn wah teh-goh-roh dehss kah?

Have you a room with bath?

Furotsuki no heya ga arimasu ka?

Foo-roht-soo-kee noh heh-yah gah ah-ree-mahss kah?

10

for one person.
hitori sama.
hee-toh-ree sah-mah.

for two.
futari sama.
foo-tah-ree sah-mah.

for one night.
hito ban (or) ippaku.
hee-toh bahn eep-pah-koo.

for four days.
yokka kan.
yohk-kah kahn.

for a week.
itshū kan hodo.
eet-SHOO kahn hoh-doh.

I shall be here until Monday.
Watakushi wa getsuyō made taizai itashimasu.
Wah-tahk-shee wah geht-soo-YOH mah-deh tah'ee-zah'ee ee-tah-shee-mahss.

Tuesday.
Kayōbi.
Kah-YOH-bee.

Wednesday.
Suiyōbi.
Soo'ee-YOH-bee.

Thursday.
Mokuyōbi.
Moh-koo-YOH-bee.

Friday.
Kinyōbi.
Keen-YOH-bee.

Saturday.
Doyōbi.
Doh-YOH-bee.

Sunday.
Nichiyōbi.
Nee-chee-YOH-bee.

Please mail this.
Kore wo okutte kudasai.
Koh-reh woh oh-koot-teh koo-dah-sah'ee.

Is there any mail for me?
Watakushi ni tegami ga kiteimasu ka?
Wah-tahk-shee nee teh-gah-mee gah kee-teh'ee-mahss kah?

I need an interpreter.
Watakushi wa tsūyaku ga hitsuyō desu.
Wah-tahk-shee wah TSOO-*yah-koo gah heet-soo-*
YOH *dehss.*

a secretary.	**a guide.**
hiso.	gaido.
hee-soh.	*gah'ee-doh.*

Are there any packages for me?
Watakushi ni kozutsumi ga kiteimasu ka?
Wah-tahk-shee nee koh-zoot-soo-mee gah kee-
teh'ee-mahss kah?

My key, please.
Watakushi no kagi o kudasai.
Wah-tahk-shee noh kah-ghee oh koo-dah-sah'ee.

stamps.	**writing paper.**	**an envelope.**
kitte.	binsen.	fūtō.
kit-teh.	*been-sehn.*	FOO-TOH.

How much is it?
Ikura desu ka?
Ee-koo-rah dehss kah?

The room is too small.
Kono heya wa chiisa sugimasu.
Koh-noh heh-yah wah chee'ee-sah soo-ghee-mahss.

too noisy.
yakamashi sugimasu.
yah-kah-mah-shee soo-ghee-mahss.

very good.	**bad.**
taihen kekko desu.	warui.
tah'ee-hehn keh-koh dehss.	*wah-roo'ee.*

Are the meals included?
 Shokuji komi desu ka?
 Shoh-koo-jee koh-mee dehss kah?

Is breakfast included?
 Chōshoku komi desu ka?
 CHO-*shoh-koo koh-mee dehss kah?*

Where is the telephone?
 Denwa wa doko ni arimasu ka?
 Dehn-wah wah doh-koh nee ah-ree-mahss kah?

NOTE: The standard expression for answering the telephone is "moshi moshi," and this useful expression can be used in any circumstance for attracting someone's attention, such as hotel personnel, waitresses, taxi drivers, etc.

Where is the bathroom?
 Furoba wa doko ni arimasu ka?
 Foo-roh-bah wah doh-koh nee ah-ree-mahss kah?

   the toilet?   **Is there a shower?**
    benjo?   Shawa tsuki desu ka?
    behn-joh?   *Shah-wah tsoo-kee dehss kah?*

Please send the chambermaid.
 Jochū-san wo yonde kudasai.
 *Joh-*CHOO-*sahn woh yohn-deh koo-dah-sah'ee.*

Please have this cleaned.
 Kore wo kurining ni dashite kudasai.
 Koh-reh woh koo-ree-neeng nee dahsh-teh koo-dah-sah'ee.

I want it pressed only.
Airon dake kakete kudasai.
Ah'ee-rohn dah-keh kah-keh-teh koo-dah-sah'ee.

Please wash this.
Kore wo sentaku shite kudasai.
Koh-reh woh sehn-tah-koo shee-teh koo-dah-sah'ee.

I need it for tonight.
Kore wa konban made ni hitsuyō desu.
Koh-reh wah kohn-bahn mah-deh nee heet-soo-YOH dehss.

> **for tomorrow.**
> asu made.
> *ah-soo mah-deh.*

How long will it take?
Dono kurai kakarimasu ka?
Doh-noh koo-rah'ee kah-kah-ree-mahss kah?

Is it certain?
Sore wa tashika desu ka?
Soh-reh wah tah-shee-kah dehss kah?

I want these shoes shined.
Kono kutsu wo migaite kudasai.
Koh-noh koot-soo woh mee-gah'ee-teh koo-dah-sah'ee.

What time is lunch?
Chūshoku wa nan ji goro desu ka?
CHOO-shoh-koo wah nahn jee goh-roh dehss kah?

What time is dinner?
Yūshoku wa nan ji goro desu ka?
Yoo-shoh-koo wah nahn jee goh-roh dehss kah?

Please bring towels.
Taoru wo motte kite kudasai.
Tah-oh-roo woh moht-teh kee-teh koo-dah-sah'ee.

Please bring soap.
Sekken wo motte kite kudasai.
Sehk-kehn woh moht-teh kee-teh koo-dah-sah'ee.

The water is not hot.
Oyu wa atsuku arimasen.
Oh-yoo wah aht-soo-koo ah-ree-mah-sehn.

I would like some cigarettes.
Watakushi wa shigaretto ga hoshii desu.
Wah-tahk-shee wah shee-gah-reht-toh gah hoh-shee'ee dehss.

Give me matches, please.
Matchi wo kudasai.
Mah-tchee woh koo-dah-sah'ee.

This does not work.
Kore wa koshō shite imasu.
Koh-reh wah koh-SHOH shee-teh ee-mahss.

Bellboy!	**Ice, please.**
Boi-san!	Kōri wo kudasai.
Boh'ee-sahn!	*KOH-ree woh koo-dah-sah'ee.*

Please bring my breakfast to my room.
Chōshoku wo heya made hakonde kudasai.
CHOH-shoh-koo woh heh-yah mah-deh hah-kohn-deh koo-dah-sah'ee.

Orange juice, rolls and coffee.
Orenji jusu to pan to cōhi.
Oh-rehn-jee joo-soo toh pahn toh KOH-hee.

Some butter, please.
> Bata wo onegai shimasu.
> *Bah-tah woh oh-neh-gah'ee shee-mahss.*

Bacon and eggs.
> Bēkon to tamago.
> *BEH-kohn toh tah-mah-goh.*

My bill, please.
> Kanjogaki wo kudasai.
> *Kahn-joh-gah-kee woh koo-dah-sah'ee.*

Is everything all right?
> Zenbu fukumarete imasu ka?
> *Zehn-boo foo-koo-mah-reh-teh ee-mahss kah?*

Let's go.
> Ikimasho.
> *Ee-kee-mah-shoh.*

Here are some typical answers that people in the hotel may make to you in reply to your questions:

There is not any.
> Nani mo arimasen.
> *Nah-nee moh ah-ree-mah-sehn.*

There is a letter for you.
> Anata ni otegami ga kiteimasu.
> *Ah-nah-tah nee oh-teh-gah-mee gah kee-teh'ee-mahss.*

Nobody came.
> Donata mo irasshaimasen deshita.
> *Doh-nah-tah moh ee-rahs-shah'ee-mah-sehn dehsh-tah.*

Nobody called.

Donata mo oyobishimasen deshita.

Doh-nah-tah moh oh-yoh-bee-shee-mah-sehn dehsh-tah.

A gentleman wants to see you.

Otoko no okyaku-sama ga anata ni gomenkai desu.

Oh-toh-koh noh ohk-yah-koo-sah-mah gah ah-nah-tah nee goh-mehn-kah'ee dehss.

A lady wants to see you.

Onnano no okyaku-sama ga anata ni gomenkai desu.

Ohn-nah-noh noh ohk-yah-koo-sah-mah gah ah-nah-tah nee goh-mehn-kah'ee dehss.

When meeting or leaving friends don't forget to bow, since this is the custom of the country. And here are some expressions of general greeting for you to review:

Good morning.

Ohayō gozaimasu.

Oh-high-YOH goh-zah'ee-mahss.

> (This is a more polite form than "Ohayō" by itself.)

Good day or **Good afternoon.**

Konnichiwa

Koh-nee-chee-wah.

Good evening.

Konbanwa.

Kohn-bahn-wah.

Good-by.

Sayōnara.

Sah-YOH-nah-rah.

Note that when you are paying hotel bills, some higher mathematics is called for. Here are the numbers in the hundreds:

100
  hyaku
  h'yah-koo

200
  nihyaku
  nee-h'yah-koo

300
  sanbyaku
  sahn-b'yah-koo

400
  yohnyaku
  yoh-n'yah-koo

500
  gohyaku
  goh-h'yah-koo

600
  roppyaku
  rohp-p'yah-koo

700
  nanahyaku
  nah-nah-h'yah-koo

800
  happyaku
  hahp-p'yah-koo

900
  kyuhyaku
  k'yoo-h'yah-koo

1000
  sen
  sehn

HERE'S HOW TO TELL TIME:

What time is it, please?
  Dōzo nan ji, desu ka?
  Doh-zoh nahn jee, dehss kah?

It is one o'clock.
  Ichi ji desu.
  Ee-chee jee dehss.

> **One twenty-five.**
>   Ichi ji nijūgo fun.
>   *Ee-chee jee nee-joo-goh foon.*

half past one.
  ichi ji han.
  ee-chee jee hahn.

a quarter to two.
  ni ji jūgo fun mae.
  nee jee JOO-*goh foon mah-eh.*

five to two.
  ni ji go fun mae.
  nee jee goh foon mah-eh.

exactly two o'clock.
  chōdo ni ji.
  CHOH-*doh nee jee.*

noon.
  shōgo.
  SHOH-*goh.*

midnight.
  mayonaka.
  mah-yoh-nah-kah.

at three in the afternoon.
  gogo san ji ni.
  goh-goh sahn jee nee.

at eight in the morning.
  gozen hachi ji ni.
  goh-zehn hah-chee jee nee.

at nine in the evening.
  gogo ku ji ni.
  goh-goh koo jee nee.

IV

WHEN YOU ARE HUNGRY

Sukiyaki, a delicious combination of meat, bean-curd and vegetables cooked while you watch, has become increasingly familiar to Americans in recent years. But there are many other good things to eat in Japan. Here are some expressions to help you in your culinary explorations.

Where is a good restaurant?
    Yoi restoran wa doko desu ka?
    Yoh-ee rehs-toh-rahn wah doh-koh dehss kah?

("Restoran" refers to a "Western-style" restaurant, while "ryori-ya" would indicate a Japanese-style restaurant.)

A table for four, please.
Yonin no teburu wo onegai shimasu.
*Yoh-neen noh teh-boo-roo woh oh-neh-gah'ee
shee-mahss.*

What do you recommend?
Nani ga oishii desu ka?
Nah-nee gah oh-ee-shee'ee dehss kah?

Bring us this, please.
Watakushitachi ni kore wo motte kite kudasai.
*Wah-tahk-shee-tah-chee nee koh-reh woh moht-
teh kee-teh koo-dah-sah'ee.*

Two orders of this and one of that.
Kore wo ninin mae to are wo ichinin mae onegai
shimasu.
*Koh-reh woh nee-neen mah-eh toh ah-reh woh
ee-chee-neen mah-eh oh-neh-gah'ee shee-mass.*

Bring me, please...
...wo motte kite kudasai.
...woh moht-teh kee-teh koo-dah-sah'ee.

fish soup.
sakana sūpu.
sah-kah-nah soo-*poo.*

raw fish.
sashimi.
sah-shee-mee.

roast beef.
rōsuto bīfu.
ROHS-*toh* BEE-*foo.*

steak.
suteiki.
soo-teh'ee-kee.

rare.
nama yaki.
nah-mah yah-kee.

medium.
  chu yaki.
  choo yah-kee.

well done.
  yoku yaite.
  yoh-koo yah'ee-teh.

oysters.
  kaki.
  kah-kee.

lobster.
  ise ebi.
  ee-seh eh-bee.

mutton.
  hitsuji no niku.
  hit-soo-jee noh nee-koo.

ham.
  hamu.
  hah-moo.

roast pork.
  rōsuto poku.
  ROHS-*toh poh-koo.*

beef.
  gyūniku.
  g'YOO-nee-koo.

fried shrimps.
  tenpura.
  tehn-poo-rah.

soy sauce.
  soyu.
  soh-yoo.

mustard.
  karashi.
  kah-rah-shee.

rice cracker.
  senbei.
  sehn-beh'ee.

pickles.
  tsukemono.
  tsoo-keh-moh-noh.

boiled rice.
  gohan.
  goh-hahn

dried seaweed.
  nori.
  noh-ree.

salad.
  sarada.
  sah-rah-dah.

vegetable.
  yasai.
  yah-sah'ee.

omelet.
  omuretsu.
  oh-moo-reht-soo.

fried eggs.
  medamayaki.
  meh-dah-mah-yah-kee.

soft boiled eggs.
  hanjuku tamago.
  hahn-joo-koo tah-mah-goh.

hard boiled eggs.   **rolls.**
  yude tamago.   roru pan.
  yoo-deh tah-mah-goh.   *roh-roo pahn.*

fried chicken.
  tori no furai.
  toh-ree noh foo-rah'ee.

salmon.   **cucumbers.**   **shrimps.**
  sāke.   kyuri.   ebi.
  SAH-*keh.*   *k'yoo-ree.*   *eh-bee.*

onions.   **peas.**
  tamanegi.   endo mame.
  tah-mah-neh-ghee.   *ehn-doh mah-meh.*

string beans.   **carrots.**   **spinach.**
  ingen.   ninjin.   horenso.
  een-gehn.   *neen-jeen.*   *hoh-rehn-soh.*

And here are some tasty Japanese specialties:

bean soup.   **beef sukiyaki.**
  misoshiru.   gyuniku sukiyaki.
  mee-soh-shee-roo.   *g'yoo-nee-koo s'kee-yah-kee.*

boiled chicken with vegetables and spiced sauce.
  tori no mizutaki.
  toh-ree noh mee-zoo-tah-kee.

What have you for dessert?
  Desāto wa nani ga arimasu ka?
  *Deh-*SAH-*toh wah nah-nee gah ah-ree-mahss kah?*

Bring us some coffee now, please.
Kohee wo ima onegai shimasu.
Koh-hee woh ee-mah oh-neh-gah'ee shee-mahss.

tea.	lemon.	milk.
ocha.	remon.	gyunyu.
oh-chah.	*reh-mohn.*	*g'yoon-yoo.*

sugar.	bread.	butter.	salt.
sato.	pan.	bata.	shio.
sah-toh.	*pahn.*	*bah-tah.*	*shee-oh.*

pepper.	vinegar.	oil.
kosho.	su.	abura.
koh-shoh.	*soo.*	*ah-boo-rah.*

cake.	fruit.
keiku.	kudamono.
keh'ee-koo.	*koo-dah-moh-noh.*

grapes.	a peach.	a pear.
budo.	momo.	nashi.
boo-doh.	*moh-moh.*	*nah-shee.*

Please bring me another fork.
Hokano fōku wo motte kite kudasai.
Hoh-kah-noh FOH-koo woh moht-teh kee-teh koo-dah-sah'ee.

knife.	plate.	napkin.
naifu.	sara.	napukin.
nah'ee-foo.	*sah-rah.*	*nahp-kin.*

spoon.	chopsticks.	match.
saji.	hashi.	matchi.
sah-jee.	*hah-shee.*	*mah-tchee.*

More beer, please.
  Motto bīru wo onegai shimasu.
  Moht-toh BEE-*roo woh oh-neh-gah'ee shee-mahss.*

Another glass of water, please.
  Mō ippai mizu wo kudasai.
  Мон *eep-pah'ee mee-zoo woh koo-dah-sah'ee.*

whisky.	**cocktail.**
uisukī.	kakuteru.
*oo'ees-*KEE.	*kah-koo-teh-roo.*

mineral water.	**sherry.**	**brandy.**
tansansui.	sherī.	burandē.
tahn-sahn-swee.	*sheh-*REE.	*brahn-*DEH.

sake (Japanese liquor made from rice).
  sake.
  sah-keh.

Bring the check, please.
  Kanjō wo kudasai.
  *Kahn-*JOH *woh koo-dah-sah'ee.*

Is the tip included?
  Chippu wa fukumarete imasu ka?
  Cheep-poo wah foo-mah-reh-teh ee-mahss kah?

Here, this is for you.
  Hai, kore wa anata no desu.
  High, koh-reh wah ah-nah-tah noh dehss.

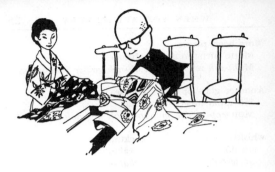

V

WHEN YOU GO SHOPPING

In visiting Japanese shops remember to use the salutations you have learned upon entering and upon leaving.

This extra politeness will secure better relations for you. Here are the words and expressions you will most frequently use:

How much is this?
> Kore wa ikura desu ka?
> *Koh-reh wah ee-koo-rah dehss kah?*

How much is that?
> Are wa ikura desu ka?
> *Ah-reh wah ee-koo-rah dehss kah?*

I like this one.
Watakushi wa kore ga suki desu.
Wah-tahk-shee wah koh-reh gah soo-kee dehss.

I like that one more.
Watakushi wa ano hō ga suki desu.
Wah-tahk-shee wah ah-noh ноН gah soo-kee dehss.

I do not like this color.
Watakushi wa kono iro wa amari suki dewa
arimasen.
Wah-tahk-shee wah koh-noh ee-roh wah ah-mah-ree soo-kee deh-wah ah-ree-mah-sehn.

I want green.
Midori iro ga hoshii no desu.
Mee-doh-ree ee-roh gah hoh-shee'ee noh dehss.

white.	**black.**	**yellow.**
shiro.	kuro.	kiiro.
shee-roh.	*koo-roh.*	*kee'ee-roh.*

pink.	**red.**	**brown.**
momo iro.	aka.	chairo.
moh-moh ee-roh.	*ah-kah.*	*chah-ee-roh.*

blue.	**purple.**
ao.	murasaki.
ah-oh.	*moo-rah-sah-kee.*

This is too expensive.
Kore wa taka sugimasu.
Koh-reh wah tah-kah soo-ghee-mahss.

Something cheaper, please.
Nanika motto yasui shinamono wo onegai shimasu.
Nah-nee-kah moht-toh yah-swee shee-nah-moh-noh woh oh-neh-gah'ee shee-mahss.

I will give you 100 yen for it.
Watakushi wa sore wo hyaku-en de kaimashu.
*Wah-tahk-shee wah soh-reh woh h'yah-koo-ehn
deh kah-ee-mahsh.*

I shall take it with me.
Watakushi wa sore wo motte ikimasu.
*Wah-tahk-shee wah soh-reh woh moht-teh ee-kee-
mahss.*

Please pack it.
Tsutsunde kudasai.
Tsoo-tsoon-deh koo-dah-sah'ee.

Send it to the Dai-ichi Hotel, please.
Dai-ichi hoteru e okutte kudasai.
*Dah'ee-ee-chee hoh-teh-roo eh oh-koot-teh koo-
dah-sah'ee.*

I would like a hat.
Bōshi ga hoshii no desu ga.
BOH-*shee gah hoh-shee'ee noh dehss gah.*

gloves.	**leather.**
tebukuro.	kawa.
teh-boo-koo-roh.	*kah-wah.*

suit.	**jacket.**	**necktie.**
sūtsu.	uwagi.	nekutai.
SOOT-*soo.*	*oo-wah-ghee.*	*neh-koo-tah'ee.*

shirt.	**belt.**	**underwear.**
waishatsu.	bando.	shitagi.
wah'ee-shah-tsoo.	*bahn-doh.*	*shee-tah-ghee.*

socks.	**shoes.**
kutsushita.	kutsu.
koot-soo-shee-tah.	*koot-soo*

skirt.
  sukāto.
  SOO-KAH-*toh.*

blouse.
  burausu.
  boo-rah-ooss.

sweater.
  suetā.
  *sweh-*TAH.

scarf.
  erimaki.
  eh-ree-mah-kee.

dress.
  doresu.
  doh-rehss.

slip.
  suripu.
  soo-ree-poo.

brassiere.
  burajā.
  *boo-rah-*JAH.

panties.
  pantee.
  pahn-tee.

stockings.
  naga kutsushita.
  nah-gah koot-soo-shee-tah.

Have you a cotton blouse?
Momen no burausu ga arimashu ka?
Moh-mehn noh boo-rah-ooss gah ah-ree-mahsh kah?

I want one in rayon.
Reiyon no wo hitotsu onegai shimasu.
Reh'ee-yohn noh woh hee-toht-soo oh-neh-gah'ee shee-mahss.

Is this hand-sewn?
Kore wa tenui desu ka?
Koh-reh wah teh-nwee dehss kah?

Is this imported?
Kore wa yunyūhin desu ka?
*Koh-reh wah yoo-n'*YOO-*heen dehss kah?*

Is this domestic?
Kore wa kokusanhin desu ka?
Koh-reh wah koh-koo-sahn-heen dehss kah?

The sleeves are too long.
    Sode ga naga sugimasu.
    Soh-deh gah nah-gah soo-ghee-mahss.

The sleeves are too short.
    Sode ga mijika sugimasu.
    Soh-deh gah mee-jee-kah soo-ghee-mahss.

I want the skirt narrower.
    Hosome no sukato ga hoshii desu.
    *Hoh-soh-meh noh soo-kah-toh gah hoh-shee'ee
        dehss.*

It is for a gentleman.
    Kore wa shinshi yo.
    Koh-reh wah sheen-shee yoh.

It is for a lady.
    Kore wa fujin yo desu.
    Koh-reh wah foo-jeen yoh dehss.

About this size. (with gestures!)
    Kono gurai no saizu desu.
    Koh-noh goo-rah'ee noh sah'ee-zoo dehss.

> **too short.**
>   mijika sugimasu.
>   *mee-jee-kah soo-ghee-mahss.*

> **like this.**   **too long.**
>   kono yo ni.   naga sugimasu.
>   *koh-noh yoh nee.*   *nah-gah soo-ghee-mahss.*

> **too big.**
>   ōki sugimasu.
>   OH-*kee soo-ghee-mahss.*

It is too small.
Chisai sugimasu.
Chee-sah'ee soo-ghee-mahss.

May I try this on?
Kore wo kite mite mo ii desu ka?
*Koh-reh woh kee-teh mee-teh moh ee-ee dehss
kah?*

I want to buy a watch.
Watakushi wa tokei wo kaitai no desu ga.
*Wah-tahk-shee wah toh-keh'ee woh kah'ee-tah'ee
noh dehss gah.*

a bracelet. udewa. *oo-deh-wah.*	**a ring.** yubiwa. *yoo-bee-wah.*
earrings. mimiwa. *mee-mee-wah.*	**a necklace.** kubiwa. *koo-bee-wah.*
handbag. hando baggu. *hahn-doh bah-goo.*	**pearls.** shinju. *shin-joo.*
silver compact. gin no konpakuto. *ghin noh kohn-pahk-toh.*	**dolls.** ningyō. *neen-g'YOH.*

lacquer ware.
urushi no nurimono.
oo-roo-shee noh noo-ree-moh-noh.

pottery. tōki. *TOH-kee.*	**(Japanese) color prints.** hanga. *hahn-gah.*

porcelain ware.
setomono.
seh-toh-moh-noh.

some pure silk.
kinuji.
kee-noo-jee.

some crepe.
chirimen.
chee-ree-mehn.

scroll.
kakejuku.
kah-keh-joo-koo.

I am just looking around.
Tada mite iru dake desu.
Tah-dah mee-teh ee-roo dah-keh dehss.

I shall come back tomorrow.
Ashita mata kimasu.
Ah-shee-tah mah-tah kee-mahss.

I will return later.
Nochi hodo mata kimasu.
Noh-chee hoh-doh mah-tah kee-mahss.

I would like to buy some post cards.
Hagaki ga kaitai desu.
Hah-gah-kee gah kah'ee-tah'ee dehss.

This is beautiful.
Kore wa kirei desu.
Koh-reh wah kee-reh'ee dehss.

I would like to buy a map of the city.
Watakushi wa machi no chizu ga kaitai desu.
*Wah-tahk-shee wah mah-chee noh chee-zoo gah
kah'ee-tah'ee dehss.*

I would like to buy an English language guide book.
Eigo no annaisho wo kaitai desu.
*Eh'ee-goh noh ahn-nah'ee-shoh woh kah'ee-tah'ee
dehss.*

Send these flowers to _____.
Kono hana wo _____ e okutte kudasai.
Koh-noh hah-nah woh _____ eh oh-koot-teh koo-dah-sah'ee.

I would like to buy toothpaste.
Hamigaki ga kaitai desu.
Hah-mee-gah-kee gah kah'ee-tah'ee dehss.

a toothbrush.	**cold cream.**	
ha burashu.	kōrudo kurīmu.	
hah brahsh.	KOH-*roo-doh* koo-REE-*moo*	

powder.	**a lipstick.**	
oshiroi.	kuchibeni.	
oh-shee-roh'ee.	*koo-chee-beh-nee.*	

needles.	**pins.**	**thread.**
hari.	pin.	ito.
hah-ree.	*pin.*	*ee-toh.*

bandages.	**cotton pads.**
hōtai.	dasshimen.
HOH-*tah'ee.*	*dahs-shee-mehn.*

aspirin.	**sunglasses.**
asupurin.	iromegane.
ahss-poo-reen.	*ee-roh-meh-gah-neh.*

razor blades.
kamisori no ha.
kah-mee-soh-ree noh hah.

shaving soap.
higesori yō no sekken.
hee-gheh-soh-ree YOH *noh sehk-kehn.*

cigarettes.	**cigars.**
shigaretto.	hamoki.
shee-gah-reht-toh.	*hah-moh-kee.*

tobacco.
  paipu tabako.
  pah'ee-poo tah-bah-koh.

camera film.
  shashin no fuirumu.
  shah-sheen noh foo'ee-roo-moo.

I would like these pictures developed.
  Kono shashin wo genzo shite kudasai.
  Koh-noh shah-sheen woh ghehn-zoh shee-teh koo-dah-sah'ee.

  for tomorrow.
    myonichi made ni.
    m'yoh-nee-chee mah-deh nee.

When should I come back?
  Itsu o ukagi shitara yoroshii desu ka?
  It-soo oh oo-kah-ghee shee-tah-rah yoh-roh-shee'ee dehss ka?

And here are some replies that salespeople may make to you:

May I help you, sir?
  Nani ka goyō desu ka?
  Nah-nee kah goh-YOH dehss kah?

What do you wish, madam?
  Okusama nani ka goyō desu ka?
  Oh-koo-sah-mah nan-nee kah goh-YOH dehss kah?

What size, please?
Dono saizu ni shimasu ka?
Doh-noh sah'ee-zoo nee shee-mahss kah?

What color do you wish?
Dono iro ga okonomi desu ka?
Doh-noh ee-roh gah oh-koh-noh-mee dehss kah?

Will you take it with you?
Gojibun de omochi kaeri ni narimasu ka?
Goh-jee-boon deh oh-moh-chee kah-eh-ree nee nah-ree-mahss kah?

Shall we send it?
Ookuri shimashō ka?
Oh-oh-koo-ree shee-mah-SHOH kah?

What is your address?
Gojūsho wa dochira desu ka?
Goh-JOO-shoh wah doh-chee-rah dehss kah?

We have none.
Gozaimasen.
Goh-zah'ee-mah-sehn.

Here is your change.	**Here is your receipt.**
Otsuri desu.	Uketori desu.
Oht-soo-ree dehss.	*Oo-keh-toh-ree dehss.*

It is not possible.
Sore wa dekimasen.
Soh-reh wah deh-kee-mah-sehn.

Come again.
Mata oide kudasai.
Mah-tah oh-ee-deh koo-dah-sah'ee.

VI

WHEN YOU GO SIGHT-SEEING

As you visit the scenic and man-made wonders
of Japan, don't hesitate to use the expressions
in this chapter, as well as those you have already
learned, in speaking to all local people you may
encounter: guides, custodians, policemen and
even passers-by. They will be flattered by your
interest in their cultural heritage, and you will
take home interesting memories of even short
language contacts with people you meet.

What are the points of interest here?
 Koko wa donna ten ga kyōmi ga arimasu?
 *Koh-koh wah dohn-nah tehn gah k'YOH-mee gah
   ah-ree-mahss?*

36

Is this a temple?

Kore wa o-tera desu ka?

Koh-reh wah oh-teh-rah dehss kah?

May I go in?

Hairu koto ga dekimasu ka?

Hah'ee-roo koh-toh gah deh-kee-mahss kah?

Where is the Tokyo tower?

Tōkyō tawā wa doko desu ka?

Toh-k'yoh tah-wah wah doh-koh dehss kah?

Please direct me to the Kabuki Theater.

Kabukiza e annai shite kudasai.

Kah-boo-kee-zah eh ahn-nah'ee shee-teh koo-dah-sah'ee.

Please speak more slowly.

Motto yukkuri hanashite kudasai.

Moht-toh yook-koo-ree hah-nah-shee-teh koo-dah-sah'ee.

Please show me the most important sights.

Omona meisho wo misete kudasai.

Oh-moh-nah meh'ee-shoh woh mee-seh-teh koo-dah-sah'ee.

Please repeat.

Mō ichido kurikaeshite kudasai.

Moh ee-chee-doh koo-ree-kah-eh-shee-teh koo-dah-sah'ee.

Where are the theaters located?

Gekijō wa doko deshō ka?

Geh-kee-joh wah doh-koh deh-shoh kah?

Which is the principal shopping street?
Omona shōtengai wa doko desu ka?
Oh-moh-nah SHOH-*tehn-gah'ee wah doh-koh dehss kah?*

castle.	shrine.
shiro.	jinja.
shee-roh.	*jeen-jah.*

Where is the museum?
Hakubutsukan wa doko desu ka?
Hahk-boot-soo-kahn wah doh-koh dehss kah?

Is the museum open now?
Hakubutsukan wa ima aite imasu ka?
Hahk-boot-soo-kahn wah ee-mah ah'ee-teh ee-mahss kah?

What is the admission?
Nyūjōryō wa ikura desu ka?
*N'*YOO-JOH-*r'*YOH *wah ee-koo-rah dehss kah?*

Is the admission free?
Nyūjōryō wa muryō desu ka?
*N'*YOO-JOH-*r'*YOH *wah moo-r'*YOH *dehss kah?*

Is it all right to take pictures?
Shashin wo totte mo yoroshii desu ka?
Shah-shin woh toht-teh moh yoh-roh-shee'ee dehss kah?

Is it open on Sundays?
Nichiyōbi wa aite imasu ka?
*Nee-chee-*YOH-*bee wah ah'ee-teh ee-mahss kah?*

This is very beautiful.
Kore wa taihen kirei desu.
Koh-reh wah tah'ee-hehn kee-ray'ee dehss.

How old is this?
   Kore wa nannen gurai furui desu ka?
   Koh-reh wah nahn-nehn goo-rah'ee foo-roo'ee
     dehss kah?

When was it built?
   Kore wa itsugoro tateta mono desu ka?
   Koh-reh wah eet-soo-goh-roh tah-teh-tah moh-
     noh dehss kah?

A map of the city, please.
   Shinai no chizu wo kudasai.
   Shee-nah'ee noh chee-zoo woh koo-dah-sah'ee.

Who built it?
   Dare ga tateta mono desu ka?
   Dah-reh gah tah-teh-tah moh-noh dehss kah?

Is this an original?
   Kore wa genbutsu desu ka?
   Koh-reh wah ghehn-boot-soo dehss kah?

Is the Imperial Palace far?
   Kyūjō wa tōi desu ka?
   K'yoo-joh wah toh'ee dehss kah?

What bus do I take to the Asakusa?
   Asakusa e iku ni wa dono basu ni noreba yoroshii
     desu ka?
   Ah-sah-koo-sah eh ee-koo nee wah doh-noh bahss
     nee noh-reh-bah yoh-roh-shee'ee dehss kah?

Is this a Buddhist temple?
   Kore wa Bukkyō no otera desu ka?
   Koh-reh wah Book-k'yoh noh oh-teh-rah dehss
     kah?

Is this a Shinto shrine?
  Kore wa Shintō no jinja desu ka?
  Koh-reh wah Sheen-TOH noh jeen-jah dehss kah?

Where is a Catholic church?
  Katorikku no kyōkai wa doko desu ka?
  Kah-toh-reek-koo noh k'YOH-kah'ee wah doh-koh dehss kah?

Where is a Protestant church?
  Shinkyo no kyōkai wa doko desu ka?
  Sheen-k'yoh noh k'YOH-kah'ee wah doh-koh dehss kah?

Where is a Jewish temple?
  Yudaya kyo no kyōkai wa doko desu ka?
  Yoo-dah-yah k'yoh noh k'YOH-kah'ee wah doh-koh dehss kah?

Here are some things that people may say to you when you are sight-seeing:

The admission is 100 yen.
  Nyūjōryō wa hyaku-en desu.
  N'YOO-JOH-r'YOH wah h'yah-koo-ehn dehss.

Have you a ticket?
  Kippu wo omochi desu ka?
  Kip-poo woh oh-moh-chee dehss kah?

Follow the guide.
  Gaido ni tsuite kite kudasai.
  Gah'ee-doh nee tswee-teh kee-teh koo-dah-sah'ee.

It is closed.	**It is open.**
Shimatte imasu.	Aite imasu.
Shee-maht-teh ee-mahss.	*Ah'ee-teh ee-mahss.*

No admittance.
   Nyūjō okotowari.
   N'YOO-JOH oh-koh-toh-wah-ree.

It is closed for repair.
   Shūri no tame heisa shite orimasu.
   SHOO-ree noh tah-meh hay-sah shee-teh oh-ree-mahss.

Photographs are prohibited.
   Shashin wo toru koto wa kinjirarete orimasu.
   Shah-shin woh toh-roo koh-toh wah kin-jee-rah-reh-teh oh-ree-mahss.

You may take pictures.
   Shashin wo totte mo kekkō desu.
   Shah-shin woh toht-teh moh kehk-KOH dehss.

Go right.
   Migi e itte kudasai.
   Mee-ghee eh eet-teh koo-dah-sah'ee.

Go straight ahead.
   Massugu itte kudasai.
   Mahs-soo-goo eet-teh koo-dah-sah'ee.

Go five streets and turn right.
   Gochō hodo itte migi e magatte kudasai.
   Goh-CHOH hoh-doh eet-teh mee-ghee eh mah-gaht-teh koo-dah-sah'ee.

VII

A BIT OF NIGHT LIFE

What show is playing tonight?
  Konban no shō wa nan desu ka?
  Kohn-bahn noh SHOH *wah nahn dehss kah?*

Please give me two tickets.
  Kippu wo nimai kudasai.
  Kip-poo woh nee-mah'ee koo-dah-sah'ee.

Are these good seats?
  Kore wa ii seki desu ka?
  Koh-reh wah ee-ee seh-kee dehss kah?

42

Where are these seats?
  Seki wa doko desu ka?
  Seh-kee wah doh-koh dehss kah?

Are they in the center?
  Mannaka desu ka?
  Mahn-nah-kah dehss kah?

In the rear?   **In the balcony?**
  Ushiro desu ka?   Sajiki desu ka?
  Oo-shee-roh dehss kah?   *Sah-jee-kee dehss kah?*

I want to reserve tickets for next Wednesday.
  Raishū no suiyōbi no kippu wo yoyaku shitai
    desu.
  *Rah-ee-SHOO noh swee-YOH-bee noh kip-poo woh
    yoh-yah-koo shee-tah'ee dehss.*

At what time does the last show start?
  Saishū no shō wa nan ji ni hajimarimasu ka?
  *Sah'ee-SHOO noh SHOH wah nahn jee nee hah-jee-
    mah-ree-mahss kah?*

At what time is the show over?
  Nan ji ni shō wa owarimasu ka?
  Nahn jee nee SHOH wah oh-wah-ree-mahss kah?

Call me a taxi, please.
  Takushī wo yonde kudasai.
  Tahk-SHEE woh yohn-deh koo-dah-sah'ee.

Take me to the Hibiya Hall.
  Hibiya kōkaidō made onegai shimasu.
  *Hee-bee-yah KOH-kah'ee-DOH mah-deh oh-neh-
    gah'ee shee-mahss.*

Take us to a good night club.

Johin na naito kurabu e annai shite kudasai.

Joh-heen nah nah-ee-toh koo-rah-boo eh ahn-nah'ee shee-teh koo-dah-sah'ee.

A table for two, please.

Futari bun no teburu wo onegai shimasu.

Foo-tah-ree boon noh teh-boo-roo woh oh-neh-gah'ee shee-mahss.

Is there a cover charge?

Kabā chāji wa arimasu ka?

Kah-BAH CHAH-jee wah ah-ree-mahss kah?

Is dinner served here?

Yūshoku wa koko de itadakemasu ka?

Yoo-shoh-koo wah koh-koh deh ee-tah-dah-keh-mahss kah?

What time is the next floor show?

Tsugi no furowa shō wa nan ji kara desu ka?

Tsoo-ghee noh foo-roh-wah SHOH wah nahn jee kah-rah dehss kah?

Please bring the menu.

Menyū wo motte kite kudasai.

Meh-n'YOO woh moht-teh kee-teh koo-dah-sah'ee.

May I have this dance?

Kondo odotte itadakemasu ka?

Kohn-doh oh-doht-teh ee-tah-dah-keh-mahss kah?

You dance very well.

Dansu ga ojozu desu ne.

Dahnss gah oh-joh-zoo dehss neh.

Please ask the orchestra to play "Kojo no Tsuki."
  Bando ni "Kojo no Tsuki" wo yaru yo ni tanonde
  kudasai.
  *Bahn-doh nee Koh-joh noh Tsoo-kee woh yah-roo
  yoh nee tah-nohn-deh koo-dah-sah'ee.*

How beautiful!
  Kirei desu ne!
  Kee-reh'ee dehss neh!

She is very charming.
  Kanojo wa miryokuteki desu.
  Kah-noh-joh wah mee-r'yoh-koo-teh-kee dehss.

We would like to see Geishas dance.
  Watakushitachi wa geisha no odori wo mitai no
  desu.
  *Wah-tahk-shee-tah-chee wah geh-ee-shah noh oh-
  doh-ree woh mee-tah'ee no dehss.*

NOTE ON GEISHA: The Geisha, whose functions have
sometimes been misunderstood by Western travelers,
is essentially an entertainer for parties and dinners.
The ideographs which compose the word Geisha
mean "art person," and the Geisha is trained in the
various Japanese cultural patterns of music, song,
dance, poetry and, of course, the commendable Japanese tradition of fostering the happiness of the male.

Are you enjoying yourself?
  Tanoshikatta desu ka?
  Tah-noh-shee-kaht-tah dehss kah?

The bill, please.
  Okanjō wo kudasai.
  Oh-kahn-JOH woh koo-dah-sah'ee.

VIII

WHEN YOU TRAVEL BY BUS OR TAXI

When you travel by bus, taxi or subway, you will find that conductors of a subway, buses or even taxis are rarely proficient in English and that Japanese is really necessary. Put yourself in their place. Would you expect a bus driver in your city to be able to reply in Japanese?

Does this bus go to the museum?
Kono basu wa hakubutsukan ni ikimasu ka?
Koh-noh bah-soo wah hahk-boot-soo-kahn nee ee-kee-mahss kah?

How much is the fare?
Ryōkin wa ikura desu ka?
R'yoh-kin wah ee-koo-rah dehss kah?

46

Please tell me where to get off.
  Watakushi no oriru tokoro wo oshiete kudasai.
  *Wah-tahk-shee noh oh-ree-roo toh-koh-roh woh
  oh-shee-eh-teh koo-dah-sah'ee.*

Where do I get off to go to _____?
  _____ e iku ni wa doko de oriru no desu ka?
  *_____ eh ee-koo nee wah doh-koh deh oh-ree-
  roo no dehss kah?*

I wish to go to the Ginza.
  Ginza e ikitai no desu.
  Gheen-zah eh ee-kee-tah'ee no dehss.

Where is a subway station?
  Chikatetsu no eki wa doko desu ka?
  *Chee-kah-teht-soo no eh-kee wah doh-koh dehss
  kah?*

This is my stop, isn't it?
  Watakushi no oriru tokoro wa koko desu ne?
  *Wah-tahk-shee no oh-ree-roo toh-koh-roh wah
  koh-koh dehss neh?*

Excuse me, I am getting off.
  Gomennasai orimasu.
  Goh-mehn-nah-sah'ee oh-ree-mahss.

Will it pass the Ginza?
  Ginza wo tōrimasu ka?
  Gheen-zah woh TOH-ree-mahss kah?

Is it far?
  Tooi desu ka?
  Toh-oh'ee dehss kah?

What is your rate to the airport?
Hikōjō made ikura desu ka?
*Hee-*KOH-JOH *mah-deh ee-koo-rah dehss kah?*

By the hour?
Ichi ji kan dewa?
Ee-chee jee kahn deh-wah?

By the day?
Ichi nichi dewa?
Ee-chee nee-chee deh-wah?

Are you a guide?
Gaido-san desu ka?
Gah'ee-doh-sahn dehss kah?

To the right.	**To the left.**
Migi e.	Hidari e.
Mee-ghee eh.	*Hee-dah-ree eh.*

Straight ahead.	**in front of....**
Massagu.	...no mae de.
Mah-sah-goo.	*...noh mah-eh deh.*

in back of....
...no ushiro de.
...noh oo-shee-roh deh.

Stop here.
Koko de tomete kudasai.
Koh-koh deh toh-meh-teh koo-dah-sah'ee.

Wait for me, please.
Matte kudasai.
Maht-teh koo-dah-sah'ee.

a short time.
sukoshi no aida.
soo-koh-shee noh ah'ee-dah.

Drive around the city.
Machi wo mawatte kudasai.
Mah-chee woh mah-waht-teh koo-dah-sah'ee.

Drive through the shopping district.
Shōtengai wo tōtte kudasai.
SHOH-*tehn-gah'ee woh* TOHT-*teh koo-dah-sah'ee.*

Drive through the theater district.
Gekijō-gai wo tōtte kudasai.
*Gay-kee-*JOH-*gah'ee woh* TOHT-*teh koo-dah-sah'ee.*

I want to see sumo wrestling.
Sumo wo mitai desu.
Soo-moh woh mee-tah'ee dehss.

I want to see an exhibition of judo.
Judo wo mitai desu.
Joo-doh woh mee-tah'ee dehss.

Show me the points of interest.
Omoshiroi tokoro ni annai shite kudasai.
Oh-moh-shee-roh'ee toh-koh-roh nee ahn-nah'ee
shee-teh koo-dah-sah'ee.

How much is it?
Ikura desu ka?
Ee-koo-rah dehss kah?

That is too much.
Taka sugimasu.
Tah-kah soo-ghee-mahss.

That is not the price agreed on.
Kimetta nedan dewa arimasen.
Kee-meht-tah neh-dahn deh-wah ah-ree-mah-sehn.

This is extra for you.
Kore wa anata ni tokubetsu agemasu.
*Koh-reh wah ah-nah-tah nee toh-koo-beht-soo
ah-gheh-mahss.*

Thank you for the pleasant ride.
Tanoshiku nosete itadakimashita.
*Tah-noh-shee-koo noh-seh-teh ee-tah-dah-kee-
mahsh-tah.*

Come tomorrow to my hotel at 9:30 in the morning.
Myōchō kuji han ni watakushi no hoteru ni kite
kudasai.
*M'YOH-CHOH koo-jee hahn nee wah-tahk-shee noh
hoh-teh-roo nee kee-teh koo-dah-sah'ee.*

at 3 o'clock in the afternoon.
gogo san ji ni.
goh-goh sahn jee nee.

at 8:30 in the evening.
gogo hachi ji han ni.
goh-goh hah-chee jee hahn nee.

How much will it be?
  Ikura ni narimasu ka?
  Ee-koo-rah nee nah-ree-mahss kah?

  for the whole day?
    ichi nichi-jū?
    *ee-chee nee-chee-*JOO?

  for the entire evening?
    hitoban-jū?
    *hee-toh-bahn-*JOO?

Here are a few expressions that bus and taxi drivers may say to you:

Where to?
  Dochira made?
  Doh-chee-rah mah-deh?

Get off here.
  Koko de orite kudasai.
  Koh-koh deh oh-ree-teh koo-dah-sah'ee.

The bag is extra.
  Kaban wa betsu desu.
  Kah-bahn wah beht-soo dehss.

You cannot take the bag.
  Kaban wa motte ikaremasen.
  Kah-bahn wah moht-teh ee-kah-reh-mah-sehn.

I cannot wait.
  Matemasen.
  Mah-teh-mah-sehn.

I will wait here.
  Koko de omachishiteimasu.
  Koh-koh deh oh-mah-chee-shee-teh'ee-mahss.

IX

IF YOU TRAVEL BY TRAIN

Japan is also noted for its fine railway trains which have the reputation of serving excellent food, especially fish. Whether you travel by 1st class (Itō), 2nd class (Nitō), 3rd class (Santō) or special 2nd class (Tokuni), the following expressions will be of use to you.

Where is the railroad station?
Kisha no eki wa doko desu ka?
Kee-shah noh eh-kee wah doh-koh dehss kah?

What is the fare to Nikko?
Nikko made no unchin wa ikura desu ka?
Nik-koh mah-deh noh oon-chin wah ee-koo-rah dehss kah?

I want a ticket to Kyoto.
Kyōto made no kippu wo onegai shimasu.
K'YOH-toh mah-deh noh kip-poo woh oh-neh-gah'ee shee-mahss.

One way.
Katamichi.
Kah-tah-mee-chee.

Round trip.
Ōfuku.
OH-foo-koo.

A time table, please.
Jikanhyō wo onegai shimasu.
Jee-kahn-h'YOH woh oh-neh-gah'ee shee-mahss.

Is food served on board?
Shanai de shokuji ga demasu ka?
Shah-nah'ee deh shoh-koo-jee gah deh-mahss kah?

Is there a faster train?
Motto hayai kisha ga arimasu ka?
Moht-toh hah-yah'ee kee-shah gah ah-ree-mahss kah?

Where is the ticket office?
Kippu uriba wa doko desu ka?
Kip-poo oo-ree-bah wah doh-koh dehss kah?

I want this baggage checked.
Kono tenimotsu wo ajukatte kudasai.
Koh-noh teh-nee-moht-soo woh ah-joo-kaht-teh koo-dah-sah'ee.

Please give me my baggage.
Watakushi no tenimotsu wo onegai shimasu.
Wah-tahk-shee noh teh-nee-moht-soo woh oh-neh-gah'ee shee-mahss.

Here are the checks.
Hikikaeken desu.
Hee-kee-kah-eh-kehn dehss.

Are you a porter?
Akabō-san desu ka?
*Ah-kah-*BOH*-sahn dehss kah?*

Please put this baggage on the train.
Kono tenimotsu wo kisha ni motte itte kudasai.
Koh-noh teh-nee-moht-soo woh kee-shah nee
moht-teh it-teh koo-dah-sah'ee.

These are my bags.
Kore wa watakushi no kaban desu.
Koh-reh wah wah-tahk-shee noh kah-bahn dehss.

Please put them in a taxi.
Takushī made hakonde kudasai.
*Tahk-*SHEE *mah-deh hah-kohn-deh koo-dah-sah'ee.*

How much is it for each piece?
Hitotsu ni tsuki ikura desu ka?
Hee-toht-soo nee tsoo-kee ee-koo-rah dehss kah?

Is this seat taken?
Kono seki wa aite imasu ka?
Koh-noh seh-kee wah ah'ee-teh ee-mahss kah?

What time does the train for Fukuoka leave?
Fukuoka yuki no kisha wa nan ji ni demasu ka?
Foo-koo-oh-kah yo-kee noh kee-shah wah nahn jee
nee deh-mahss kah?

What time does it arrive at Fukuoka?
Fukuoka ni wa nan ji tsuki masu ka?
Foo-koo-oh-kah nee wah nahn jee nee tsoo-kee
mahss kah?

How long do we stop here?
Donokurai teisha shite imasu ka?
Doh-noh-koo-rah'ee teh'ee-shah shee-teh ee-mahss kah?

Does the train stop at Fukuoka?
Fukuoka ni kisha shimasu ka?
Foo-koo-oh-kah nee kee-shah shee-mahss kah?

How much longer is it?
Dono kurai arimasu ka?
Doh-noh koo-rah'ee ah-ree-mahss kah?

Have I time to buy a newspaper?
Shimbun wo kau jikan ga arimasu ka?
Sheem-boon woh kah-oo jee-kahn gah ah-ree-mahss kah?

Is there a restaurant in the station?
Ekinai ni restoran ga arimasu ka?
Eh-kee-nah'ee nee reh-stoh-rahn gah ah-ree-mahss kah?

Please open the window.
Mado wo akete kudasai.
Mah-doh woh ah-keh-teh koo-dah-sah'ee.

May I smoke, madam?
Okusama, tabako wo sutte mo yoroshii deshō ka?
*Oh-koo-sah-mah, tah-bah-koh woh soot-teh moh yoh-roh-shee'ee deh-*SHOH* kah?*

Please close the window.
Mado wo shimate kudasai.
Mah-doh woh shee-mah-teh koo-dah-sah'ee.

Where is the dining car?
Shokudōsha wa doko deshō ka?
*Shoh-koo-*DOH*-shah wah doh-koh deh-*SHOH *ka?*

Please call me at six.
Roku ji ni yonde kudasai.
Roh-koo jee nee yohn-deh koo-dah-sah'ee.

Why is the train stopping?
Kisha wa dō shite tomatte iruno desu ka?
Kee-shah wah DOH *shee-teh toh-maht-teh ee-roo-
noh dehss kah?*

What is the matter?
Dō shita no desu ka?
DOH *shee-tah noh dehss kah?*

Where is the conductor?
Shashō wa doko desu ka?
*Shah-*SHOH *wah doh-koh dehss kah?*

Here are some things the conductor or ticket
agent may say to you:

When do you wish to leave?
Itsu otachi ni narimashu ka?
It-soo oh-tah-chee nee nah-ree-mahsh kah?

Which train?
Dō no kisha desu ka?
DOH *noh kee-shah dehss kah?*

One way or round trip?
Katamichi desu ka ofuku desu ka?
*Kah-tah-mee-chee dehss kah oh-foo-koo dehss
kah?*

There is no train today.
Kyo wa kisha ga hashitte orimasen.
K'yoh wah kee-shah gah hah-sheet-teh oh-ree-
mah-sehn.

All aboard!
Minasan gojōsha kudásai!
Mee-nah-sahn goh-JOH-shah koo-dah-sah'ee!

We will be here only ten minutes.
Watakushitachi wa juppun hodo koko ni orimasu.
Wah-tahk-shee-tah-chee wah joop-poon hoh-doh
koh-koh nee oh-ree-mahss.

You cannot get off here.
Koko de oriru koto wa dekimasen.
Koh-koh deh oh-ree-roo koh-toh wah deh-kee-
mah-sehn.

The train does not stop at Atami.
Kisha wa atami ni tomarimasen.
Kee-shah wah ah-tah-mee nee toh-mah-ree-mah-
sehn.

You must change trains.
Onorikae kudasai.
Oh-noh-ree-kah-eh koo-dah-sah'ee.

We are 15 minutes late.
Jūgo fun okurete imasu.
Joo-goh foon oh-koo-reh-teh ee-mahss.

We are on time.
Jikan dōri desu.
Jee-kahn DOH-ree dehss.

X

IF YOU TRAVEL BY CAR

Remember that you buy gasoline by the liter (about a quart) and not by the gallon. The following expressions are essential for motoring:

Fill it up.
　Ippai ni.
　Eep-pah'ee nee.

Gasoline.
　Gasorin.
　Gah-soh-reen.

Put in 30 liters, please.
　Sanjū rittoru irete, kudasai.
　*Sahn-*JOO *rit-toh-roo ee-reh-teh, koo-dah-sah'ee.*

I need some oil.
　Oiru wo onegaishimasu.
　Oh-ee-roo woh oh-neh-gah'ee-shee-mahss.

　　water.
　　　mizu.
　　　mee-zoo.

　　air.
　　　kūki.
　　　KOO-*kee.*

58

Look at the tires, please.
Taiya wo shirabete, kudasai.
Tah-ee-yah woh shee-rah-beh-teh koo-dah-sah'ee.

Have you a road map?
Dōro no chizu wa arimasu ka?
DOH-roh no chee-zoo wah ah-ree-mahss kah?

How far is Hakone?
Hakone made dono kurai desu ka?
Hah-koh-neh mah-deh doh-noh koo-rah'ee dehss kah?

Is this the way to Ise?
Ise yuki wa kono michi de yoroshii desu ka?
Ee-seh yoo-kee wah koh-noh mee-chee deh yoh-roh-shee'ee dehss ka?

Which is the road to Gora?
Gōra yuki wa dono michi desu ka?
GOH-rah yoo-kee wah doh-noh mee-chee dehss kah?

Can we get to Kyōto by evening?
Yugata made ni Kyōto ni tsukemashu ka?
Yoo-gah-tah mah-deh nee K'YOH-toh nee tsoo-keh-mahsh kah?

Is the road to Lake Ashi good?
Ashino-ko made wa ii michi desu ka?
Ah-shee-noh-koh mah-deh wah ee-ee mee-chee dehss kah?

Can you draw me a little map?
Kantan na chizu wo kaite kudasai?
Kahn-tahn nah chee-zoo woh kah'ee-teh koo-dah-sah'ee?

Is there a good restaurant in Miyanoshita?
 Miyanoshita niwa ii restoran ga arimasu ka?
 *Mee-yah-noh-shee-tah nee-wah ee-ee rehs-toh-rahn
 gah ah-ree-mahss kah?*

Is there a good hotel in Nara?
 Nara niwa ii hoteru ga arimasu ka?
 *Nah-rah nee-wah ee-ee hoh-teh-roo gah ah-ree-
 mahss kah?*

Where is the garage?
 Shako wa doko desu ka?
 Shah-koh wah doh-koh dehss kah?

Can I leave my car here?
 Jidōsha wo oite iidesu ka?
 Jee-DOH-shah woh oh'ee-teh ee-ee-dehss kah?

for a few minutes?	**all night?**
shibaraku?	yodōshi?
shee-bah-rah-koo?	*yoh-DOH-shee?*

I want the oil changed.
 Oiru no torikae wo onegai shimasu.
 *Oh'ee-roo noh toh-ree-kah'eh woh oh-neh-gah'ee
 shee-mahss.*

How much will it be?
 Ikura ni narimasu ka?
 Ee-koo-rah nee nah-ree-mahss kah?

I want my car greased.
 Jidōsha no gurīsu wo onegai shimasu.
 *Jee-DOH-shah noh goo-REESS woh oh-neh-gah'ee
 shee-mahss.*

I have a flat.
Panku shimashita.
Pan-koo shee-mahsh-tah.

Please change it.
Torikaete kudasai.
Toh-ree-kah-eh-teh koo-dah-sah'ee.

Please send a mechanic.
Shurinin no dekiru hito wo yonde kudasai.
*Shoo-ree-nin noh deh-kee-roo hee-toh woh yohn
   deh koo-dah-sah'ee.*

Are you a mechanic?
Anata wa shurinin desu ka?
Ah-nah-tah wah shoo-ree-nin dehss kah?

The car does not go.
Jidōsha ga ugokimasen.
Jee-DOH-shah gah uh-goh-kee-mah-sehn.

It has a knock.
Noku shimasu.
Noh-koo shee-mahss.

It is not running properly.
Chōshi ga yoku arimasen.
CHOH-shee gah yoh-koo ah-ree-mah-sehn.

Please examine it.
Shirabete kudasai.
Shee-rah-beh-teh koo-dah-sah'ee.

Check the spark plugs.
Tenkasen wo shirabete kudasai.
*Tehn-kah-sehn woh shee-rah-beh-teh koo-dah-
   sah'ee.*

What is the matter?
 Dō shita no desu ka?
 DOH *shee-tah noh dehss kah?*

How long will it take to fix?
 Shūri suru niwa dono kurai kakarimashu ka?
 SHOO-*ree soo-roo nee-wah doh-noh koo-rah'ee
 kah-kah-ree-mahsh kah?*

The battery is dead.
 Batterī ga nakunarimashita.
 *Bah-teh-*REE *gah nah-koo-nah-ree-mahsh-tah.*

Change the battery.
 Batterī wo torikaete kudasai.
 *Baht-teh-*REE *woh toh-ree-kah-eh-teh koo-dah-
 sah'ee.*

Charge the battery.
 Batterī wo juden shite kudasai.
 *Baht-teh-*REE *woh joo-dehn shee-teh koo-dah-
 sah'ee.*

Please wash the car.
 Jidōsha wo aratte kudasai.
 *Jee-*DOH-*shah woh ah-raht-teh koo-dah-sah'ee.*

Garage men and mechanics and helpful strangers
along the road may make some of the following
replies to you:

It is not far.
 Tōku arimasen.
 TOH-*koo ah-ree-mah-sehn.*

It's that way.
> Achira no hō desu.
> *Ah-chee-rah noh* HOH *dehss.*

Follow the road you are on.
> Ima no michi ni sotte iki nasai.
> *Ee-mah noh mee-chee nee soht-teh ee-kee nah-sah'ee.*

Turn right at the next cross-roads.
> Tsugi no yotsu kado de migi e magatte kudasai.
> *Tsoo-ghee noh yoht-soo kah-doh deh mee-ghee eh mah-gaht-teh koo-dah-sah'ee.*

Turn left beyond the bridge.
> Hashi wo koete hidari ni magatte kudasai.
> *Hah-shee woh koh-eh-teh hee-dah-ree nee mah-gaht-teh koo-dah-sah'ee.*

Go to the Miyako Restaurant.
> Miyako restoran ni itte kudasai.
> *Mee-yah-koh rehs-toh-rahn nee it-teh koo-dah-sah'ee.*

It is very good.
> Taihen ii desu.
> *Tah'ee-hehn ee-ee dehss.*

We can't fix it today.
> Shurī wa kyō dekimasen.
> *Shoo-*REE *wah k'*YOH *deh-kee-mah-sehn.*

We haven't the right parts.
> Tekitō na buhin ga arimasen.
> *Teh-kee-*TOH *nah boo-heen gah ah-ree-mah-sehn.*

We have to send for them.
> Chumon shinakerebe narimasen.
> *Choo-mohn shee-nah-keh-reh-beh nah-ree-mah-sehn.*

It will take 3 days.
> Mikka kakarimasu.
> *Meek-kah kah-kah-ree-mahss.*

I can fix it temporarily.
> Ichijiteki ni naoshimasu.
> *Ee-chee-jee-teh-kee nee nah-oh-shee-mahss.*

The carburetor needs fixing.
> Kāburēta wo shuri suru hitsuyō ga arimasu.
> *KAH-boo-REH-tah woh shoo-ree soo-roo hit-soo-YOH gah ah-ree-mahss.*

It needs new plugs.
> Atarashii puragu ga hitsuyō desu.
> *Ah-tah-rah-shee'ee poo-rah-goo gah heet-soo-YOH dehss.*

You need a new tire.
> Atarashii taiya ga hitsuyō desu.
> *Ah-tah-rah-shee'ee tah-ee-yah gah heet-soo-YOH dehss.*

battery.	fan belt.
batterī.	fan beruto.
baht-teh-REE.	*fahn beh-roo-toh.*

In case a breakdown keeps you in a small town for several days, relax. After all, you are probably on a vacation. Even if you are not, take one! Incidentally, the Japanese expression for "Take it easy!" is "Kiraku ni!"

XI

HOW TO MAKE FRIENDS

Here is an assortment of polite expressions and phrases for social use which you will find very helpful at almost any time. Remember in your social dealings to add "-san" to a person's name when addressing him or her. And don't forget to bow frequently, as the occasion demands!

I am happy to meet you.
Dōzo yoroshiku.
Doн-*zoh yoh-roh-shee-koo.*

My name is....
Watakushi wa....
Wah-tahk-shee wah....

Your name?
Anata no onamae wa?
Ah-nah-tah noh oh-nah-mah'eh wah?

This is my wife.
Watakushi no tsuma desu.
Wah-tahk-shee noh tsoo-mah dehss.

Is your wife in Tokyo?
Oku-san wa Tōkyō ni imasu ka?
Ohk-sahn wah Toh-k'yoh nee ee-mahss kah?

NOTE: Courtesy is carried so far in Japan that there are separate words for family relationships depending on whether the person is related to you or to the person to whom you are speaking; in the latter case the word used is in a more honorific category. Note the following:

(my) father.	**(your) father.**
chichi.	otō-san.
chee-chee.	*oh-TOH-sahn.*
(my) mother.	**(your) mother.**
haha.	okāsan.
hah-hah.	*oh-KAH-sahn.*
(my) older brother.	**(your) older brother.**
ami.	onī-san.
ah-mee.	*oh-NEE-sahn.*
(my) younger brother.	**(your) younger brother.**
otōto.	otōto-san.
oh-TOH-toh.	*oh-TOH-toh-sahn.*

(my) older sister.
ane.
ah-neh.

(your) older sister.
onē-san.
oh-NEH-sahn.

(my) younger sister.
imōto.
ee-MOH-toh.

(your) younger sister.
imōto-san.
ee-MOH-toh-sahn.

(my) son.
musuko.
moo-soo-koh.

(your) son.
musuko-san.
moo-soo-koh-sahn.

(my) daughter.
musume.
moo-soo-meh.

(your) daughter.
musume-san.
moo-soo-meh-sahn.

(my) husband.
shujin.
shoo-jin.

(your) husband.
go shujin.
goh shoo-jin.

(my) wife.
tsuma.
tsoo-mah.

(your) wife.
oku-san.
ohk-sahn.

fiancé(e).
iinazuke.
ee'ee-nahz-keh.

friend.
tomodachi.
toh-moh-dah-chee.

Note that "fiancé(e) and "friend" have just the one form for "yours" or "mine."

Are you familiar with the U.S.?
Anata wa America no koto ni tsuite kuwashii desu ka?
Ah-nah-tah wah Ah-meh-ree-kah noh koh-toh nee tswee-teh koo-wah-shee'ee dehss kah?

Have you been to New York?

Nyūyōrku e irasshata koto ga arimasu ka?

N'YOO-YOHR-koo ee-rahss-shah-tah koh-toh gah ah-ree-mahss kah?

Your city is very interesting.

Anata no machi wa hijō ni kyōmi ga arimasu.

Ah-nah-tah noh mah-chee wah hee-JOH nee k'YOH-mee gah ah-ree-mahss.

The garden is beautiful!

Niwa ga kirei desu ne!

Nee-wah gah kee-reh'ee dehss neh!

What a beautiful house!

Kirei na uchi desu ne!

Kee-reh'ee nah oo-chee dehss neh!

I think so.

Sō omoimasu.

SOH oh-moh'ee-mahss.

Isn't it so?

Sō deshō?

SOH deh-SHOH?

Really?

Hontō?

Hon-TOH?

Here is a picture of my wife.

Watakushi no tsuma no shashin desu.

Wah-tahk-shee noh tsoo-mah noh shah-sheen dehss.

Your daughter is very beautiful.

Anata no musume-san wa taihen kirei desu.

Ah-nah-tah noh moo-soo-meh-sahn wah tah'ee-hehn kee-reh'ee dehss.

She sings very well.

Kanojo wa taihen jōzu ni utaimasu.

Kah-noh-joh wah tah'ee-hehn JOH-zoo nee oo-tah'ee-mahss.

You dance very well.

Anata no dansu wa subarashii.

Ah-nah-tah noh dahnss wah soo-bah-rah-shee'ee.

Do you speak English?

Anata wa Eigo ga hanashimasu ka?

Ah-nah-tah wah Eh'ee-goh gah hah-nah-shee-mahss kah?

Do you like American movies?

Amerika no eiga wa suki desu ka?

Ah-meh-ree-kah noh eh'ee-gah wah soo-kee dehss kah?

Do you read books in English?

Eigo no hon wo yomimasu ka?

Eh'ee-goh noh hon woh yoh-mee-mahss kah?

Do you like to swim?

Oyogi ga suki desu ka?

Oh-yoh-ghee gah soo-kee dehss kah?

_____ **to ride horseback?**

Jōba ga _____?

JOH-bah gah _____?

_____ to go driving?
Unten ga _____?
Oon-tehn gah _____?

_____ to play tennis?
Tenisu ga _____?
Teh-nees gah _____?

_____ to play golf?
Gorufu ga _____?
Gohr-foo gah _____?

_____ to dance?
Dansu ga _____?
Dahnss gah _____?

_____ to play cards?
Kado ga _____?
Kah-doh gah _____?

(All the above should be followed by "suki desu ka" in asking questions.)

Do you like American music?
Amerika no ongaku wa suki desu ka?
Ah-meh-ree-kah noh ohn-gah-koo wah soo-kee dehss kah?

May I invite you to dance?
Dansu ni osasoi shite mo yoroshii desu ka?
Dahnss nee oh-sah-soh'ee shee-teh moh yoh-roh-shee'ee dehss kah?

I like to play tennis.
Tenisu ga suki desu.
Teh-neess gah soo-kee dehss.

Do you wish to drive?
Unten wo nasaimasu ka?
Oon-tehn woh nah-sah'ee-mahss kah?

Do you live here?
Koko ni osumai desu ka?
Koh-koh nee oh-soo-mah'ee dehss kah?

What is your address?
Gojūsho wa doko desu ka?
Goh-joo-shoh wah doh-koh dehss kah?

What is your phone number?
Anata no denwa bango wa?
Ah-nah-tah noh dehn-wah bahn-goh wah?

I am here for four days.
Watakushi wa koko ni yokkakan taizai itashi-
    mashu.
*Wah-tahk-shee wah koh-koh nee yohk-kah-kahn
    tah'ee-zah'ee ee-tah-shee-mash.*

> **two weeks.**
> nishūkan.
> *nee-SHOO-kahn.*

> **one month only.**
> hitotsuki kan dake.
> *hee-toht-soo-kee kahn dah-keh.*

Would you like a cigarette?
Shigaretto wa ikaga desu ka?
Shee-gah-reht-toh wah ee-kah-gah dehss ka?

> **A glass of wine?**
> Budōshu ippai?
> *Boo-DOH-shoo eep-pah'ee?*

anything?
  nandemo?
  nan-deh-moh?

Help yourself!
  Go jiyū ni!
  *Goh jee-*YOO *nee!*

To your health!
  Anata no gokenkō no tameni!
  *Ah-nah-tah noh goh-kehn-*KOH *noh tah-meh-nee!*

Many happy returns!
  Gochōmei wo oinori shimasu!
  *Goh-*CHOH-*may woh oh'ee-noh-ree shee-mahss!*

Congratulations!
  Omedetō!
  *Oh-meh-deh-*TOH!

With best wishes!
  Gokōfuku wo oinori shimasu!
  *Goh-*KOH-*foo-koo woh oh'ee-noh-ree shee-mahss!*

Merry Christmas!
  Kurishumasu omedetō!
  *Koo-ree-shoo-mahss oh-meh-deh-*TOH!

Happy New Year!
  Shinnen omedetō!
  *Sheen-nen oh-meh-deh-*TOH!

My sympathy.
  Godōjō mōshi agemasu.
  *Goh-*DOH-JOH MOH-*shee ah-gheh-mahss.*

Good luck!
  Go seikō wo inorimasu!
  *Goh seh'ee-*KOH *woh een-oh-ree-mahss!*

AND NOT TO FORGET ROMANCE...

When can I see you again?
  Istu omeni kakaremasu ka?
  Ees-too oh-meh-nee kah-kah-reh-mahss kah?

I think you are beautiful.
  Anata wa utsukushii to omoimasu.
  Ah-nah-tah wah oot-soo-koo-shee'ee toh oh-moh-ee-mahss.

I like you very much.
  Anata ga daisuki desu.
  Ah-nah-tah gah dah'ee-soo-kee dehss.

Do you like me?
  Watakushi ga suki desu ka?
  Wah-tahk-shee gah soo-kee dehss kah?

May I see you tomorrow?
  Myōnichi omenikakaremasu ka?
  *My'*OH-*nee-chee oh-meh-nee-kah-kah-reh-mahss kah?*

May I see you this evening?
  Konban omenikakaremasu ka?
  Kohn-bahn oh-meh-nee-kah-kah-reh-mahss kah?

Here is a present for you.
  Anata ni omiyage desu.
  Ah-nah-tah nee oh-mee-yah-gheh dehss.

I love you.

Anata wo aishimasu.

Ah-nah-tah woh ah'ee-shee-mahss.

Will you marry me?

Kekkon shite kudasaimasu ka?

Kehk-kon shee-teh koo-dah-sah'ee-mahss kah?

XII

IS THERE A DOCTOR IN THE HOUSE?

We hope that you will not get ill on your trip, but in case you need any more medical attention than an aspirin tablet, we have included this morbid little section for your edification.

Please call a doctor.
Isha wo yonde kudasai.
Ee-shah woh yohn-deh koo-dah-sah'ee.

I am ill.
Watakushi wa byōki desu.
Wah-tahk-shee wah b'YOH-kee dehss.

I have a headache.
Watakushi wa zutsu ga shimasu.
Wah-tahk-shee wah zoot-soo gah shee-mahss.

I have a bad cough.

Watakushi wa seki ga hidoi no desu.

Wah-tahk-shee wah seh-kee gah hee-doh'ee noh dehss.

I have a pain here.

Watakushi wa koko ga itamimasu.

Wah-tahk-shee wah koh-koh gah ee-tah-mee-mahss.

I have a stomach ache.

Watakushi wa i ga itai no desu.

Wah-tahk-shee wah ee gah ee-tah'ee noh dehss.

My leg hurts.

Ashi ga itai no desu.

Ah-shee gah ee-tah'ee noh dehss.

My arm hurts.

Ude ga itai no desu.

Oo-deh gah ee-tah'ee noh dehss.

My back hurts.

Senaka ga itai no desu.

Seh-nah-kah gah ee-tah'ee noh dehss.

My ear hurts.

Mimi ga itai no desu.

Mee-mee gah ee-tah'ee noh dehss.

I have chills.

Samuke ga shimasu.

Sah-moo-keh gah shee-mahss.

I have a fever.
  Netsu ga arimasu.
  Neht-soo gah ah-ree-mahss.

chest.	**head.**	**back.**
mune.	atama.	senaka.
moo-neh.	*ah-tah-mah.*	*seh-nah-kah.*

leg.	**arm.**	**shoulder.**
ashi.	ude.	kata.
ah-shee.	*oo-deh.*	*kah-tah.*

ankle.
  ashikubi.
  ah-shee-koo-bee.

Is it broken?
  Oreta no desu ka?
  Oh-reh-tah noh dehss kah?

Is it sprained?
  Suji wo chigaeta no desu ka?
  Soo-jee woh chee-gah-eh-tah noh dehss kah?

Since yesterday.
  Kino kara desu.
  Kee-noh kah-rah dehss

For twelve hours.
  Jūni ji kan mo.
  Joo-nee jee kahn moh

I have had an accident.
  Jiko ni aimashita.
  Jee-koh nee ah'ee-mahsh-tah.

I have a burn.
Yakedo wo shimashita.
Yah-keh-doh woh shee-mashsh-tah.

    a cut.
    kiriguchi.
    kee-ree-goo-chee.

    a bruise.
    uchikizu.
    oo-chee-kee-zoo.

I cannot breathe.
Kokyū ga dekimasen.
Koh-k'YOO gah deh-kee-mah-sehn.

Is it necessary to go to the hospital?
Byōin e nyūin suru hitsuyō ga arimasu ka?
*B'YOH'een eh n'YOO-een soo-roo heet-soo-YOH gah
ah-ree-mahss kah?*

What medicine is necessary?
Donna kusuri ga hitsuyō desu ka?
*Dohn-nah koo-soo-ree gah heet-soo-YOH dehss
kah?*

How often should it be taken?
Nan ji kan oki desu ka?
Nahn ji kahn oh-kee dehss ka?

How much should be taken?
Dono gurai desu ka?
Doh-noh goo-rah'ee dehss kah?

Is it necessary to stay here?
Koko ni iru koto ga hitsuyō desu ka?
*Koh-koh nee ee-roo koh-toh gah heet-soo-YOH
dehss kah?*

I am better today, thank you.
Okagesamade kyō wa yoku narimashita.
Oh-kah-geh-sah-mah-deh k'YOH wah yoh-koo nah-ree-mahsh-tah.

I have a cold.
Kaze wo hikimashita.
Kah-zeh woh hee-kee-mahsh-tah.

I have indigestion.
Shoka furyō desu.
Shoh-kah foo-r'YOH dehss.

I am nauseated.
Hakike ga shimasu.
Hah-kee-keh gah shee-mahss.

I have broken my glasses.
Megane wo kowashimashita.
Meh-gah-neh woh koh-wah-shee-mahsh-tah.

I cannot see.
Miemasen.
Mee-eh-mah-sehn.

Take this to the drugstore and wait.
Kore wo yakkyoku e motte itte matte ite kudasai.
Koh-reh woh yahk-k'yoh-koo eh moht-teh it-teh maht-teh ee-teh koo-dah-sah'ee.

Where is the drugstore?
Yakkyoku wa doko desu ka?
Yahk-k'yoh-koo wah doh-koh dehss kah?

I want some aspirin.
  Asupurin wo onegai shimasu.
  Ahss-poo-reen woh oh-neh-gah'ee shee-mahss.

> **quinine.**
>   kinīne zai.
>   *kee-NEE-neh zah'ee.*

> **iodine.**
>   yōdochinki.
>   *YOH-doh-cheen-kee.*

> **cough syrup.**
>   seki dome no shiroppu.
>   *seh-kee doh-meh noh shee-rohp-poo.*

> **drops.**
>   doroppu.
>   *doh-rohp-poo.*

And here are some things that the doctor **may** say to you:

Remove your clothes.
  Fuku wo onugi kudasai.
  Foo-koo woh oh-noo-ghee koo-dah-sah'ee.

Lie down.
  Yoko ni narinasai.
  Yoh-koh nee nah-ree-nah-sah'ee.

You must stay in bed.
  Mete inakereba ikenasen.
  Meh-teh ee-nah-keh-reh-bah ee-keh-nah-sehn.

Take this.
> Kore wo nonde kudasai.
> *Koh-reh woh nohn-deh koo-dah-sah'ee.*

>> **in water.**
>> mizu de.
>> *mee-zoo deh.*

>> **three times a day.**
>> ichi nichi ni san kai.
>> *ee-chee nee-chee nee san kah'ee.*

Open your mouth.
> Kuchi wo akete kudasai.
> *Koo-chee woh ah-keh-teh koo-dah-sah'ee.*

Inhale.   **Exhale.**
> Sutte.   Haite.
> *Soot-teh.*   *Hah'ee-teh.*

You have a temperature.
> Netsu ga arimasu.
> *Neht-soo gah ah-ree-mahss.*

I will give you an injection.
> Chūsha wo shite agemashu.
> CHOO-*shah woh shee-teh ah-gheh-mahsh.*

How long have you been ill?
> Gobyōki ni natte nagai desu ka?
> *Goh-b'YOH-kee nee naht-teh nah-gah'ee dehss kah?*

Do you feel better now?
> Ima jokibun wa yoroshii desu ka?
> *Ee-mah joh-kee-boon wah yoh-roh-shee'ee dehss kah?*

AND NOT TO FORGET THE DENTIST...

Where is there a dentist?
  Haisha wa doko desu ka?
  Hah'ee-shah wah doh-koh dehss kah?

This tooth hurts.
  Kono ha ga itami masu.
  Koh-noh hah gah ee-tah-mee mahss.

Do not extract it.
  Ha wo nukanai de kudasai.
  Hah woh noo-kah-nah'ee deh koo-dah-sah'ee.

The filling has fallen out.
  Ha no tsume mono ga toremashita.
  *Hah noh t'soo-meh moh-noh gah toh-reh-mahsh-
  tah.*

Can you fill it now?
  Ima tsumete itadakemasu ka?
  Ee-mah t'soo-meh-teh ee-tah-dah-keh-mahss kah?

  a silver filling.   **a gold filling.**
    ginkan.   kinkan.
    gheen-kahn.   *keen-kahn.*

How long will it take?
   Dono kurai kakari masu ka?
   Doh-noh koo-rah'ee kah-kah-ree mahss kah?

Please use novocaine.
   Masui wo kakete kudasai.
   Mah-swee woh kah-keh-teh koo-dah-sah'ee.

Stop!
   Yamete!
   Yah-meh-teh!

Is it permanent?
   Eijoku sei desu ka?
   Eh'ee-joh-koo seh'ee dehss kah?

Where does it hurt?
   Doko ga itami masu ka?
   Doh-koh gah ee-tah-mee mahss kah?

理髪店

XIII

AT THE BARBER'S OR BEAUTY SHOP

Don't put off getting your hair cut until you come back to the U.S.A. They are quite capable of doing it in Japan—if you tell them how you want it done. Pick out the right expression from here, throw in a little pantomime and you should have no trouble.

This will be useful for "shinshi" (gentlemen):

Is there a barber's shop near here?
　　Kono fukin de sanpatsuya wa arimasu ka?
　　Koh-noh foo-keen deh sahn-pat-soo-yah wah ah-ree-mahss kah?

84

A haircut, please.
Sanpatsu wo onegai shimasu.
Sahn-pat-soo woh oh-neh-gah'ee shee-mahss.

Not too short.
Amari mijikaku karanaide.
Ah-mah-ree mee-jee-kah-koo kah-rah-nah'ee-deh.

Not too long.
Naga sugi nai.
Nah-gah soo-ghee nah'ee.

Use clippers.
Hasami wo tsukatte kudasai.
Hah-sah-mee woh t'soo-kaht-teh koo-dah-sah'ee.

the back.	**the top.**
ushiro.	ue.
oo-shee-roh.	*oo-eh.*

Hair tonic.
Heyā tonikku.
Heh-YAH toh-neek-koo.

Cut more off the sides.
Yoko no motto kitte kudasai.
Yoh-koh noh moht-toh kit-teh koo-dah-sah'ee.

A scalp massage.	**A shampoo.**
Atama no masaki.	Shampu.
Ah-tah-mah noh mah-sah-kee.	*Sham-poo.*

A shine, please.
Kutsu migaki wo onegai shimasu.
Koot-soo mee-gah-kee woh oh-neh-gah'ee shee-mahss.

A manicure.
Manikyua.
Mah-nee-k'yoo-ah.

Is everything included?
Subete ga fukumarete orimasu ka?
Soo-beh-teh gah foo-koo-mah-reh-teh oh-ree-mahss kah?

How much is it altogether?
Minna de ikura desu ka?
Meen-nah deh ee-koo-rah dehss kah?

In this section we have not included the things
a barber may say to you, since, as in America,
barbers are naturally loquacious, and you don't
have to answer them.

This will be useful for "fujin" (ladies):

Is there a beauty salon in the hotel?
Hoteru no naka de biyōin ga arimasu ka?
*Hoh-teh-roo noh nah-kah deh bee-YOH-een gah
ah-ree-mahss kah?*

Where is there a good beauty shop?
Ii biyōin wa doko ni arimasu ka?
*Ee-ee bee-YOH-een wah doh-koh nee ah-ree-mahss
kah?*

I want my hair washed.
Kami wo araitai no desu ga.
Kah-mee woh ah-rah-ee-tah'ee noh dehss gah.

> **and set.**
> setto.
> *seht-toh.*

How long must I wait?
Dono kurai matanakereba narimasen ka?
*Doh-noh koo-rah'ee mah-tah-nah-keh-reh-bah
nah-ree-mah-sehn kah?*

I want a manicure too.
Manikyua mo onegai shimasu.
Mah-nee-k'yoo-ah moh oh-neh-gah'ee shee-mahss.

I want my hair cut.
Katto shite kudasai.
Kaht-toh shee-teh koo-dah-sah'ee.

I want my hair tinted.
Kami wo somete kudasai.
Kah-mee woh soh-meh-teh koo-dah-sah'ee.

   the same color.
      onaji iro.
      oh-nah-jee ee-roh.

   a lighter color.
      motto karui iro.
      moht-toh kah-rwee ee-roh.

   a darker color.
      motto koi iro.
      moht-toh koh'ee ee-roh.

Not so short, please.
Sonna ni mijikaku shinaide kudasai.
*Sohn-nah nee mee-jee-kah-koo shee-nah'ee-deh
koo-dah-sah'ee.*

The water is too cold.
Mizu wa taihen tsumetai.
Mee-zoo wah tah'ee-hehn t'soo-meh-tah'ee.

too hot.
atsu sugimasu.
aht-soo soo-ghee-mahss.

I part my hair here.
Watakushi wa koko de kami wo wakemasu.
*Wah-tahk-shee wah koh-koh deh kah-mee woh
wah-keh-mahss.*

I want a permanent wave.
Pamanento wo onegai shimasu.
Pah-mah-nehn-toh woh oh-neh-gah'ee shee-mahss.

XIV

DON'T BE AFRAID OF THE TELEPHONE

Many Americans are frightened by foreign telephones. Do not be afraid of them, even Japanese ones. If they are dial phones, you have nothing to worry about and, if not, simply repeat the numbers in a clear voice. For example: "Toranomon 8215 (hachi ni ichi go)."

When your phone rings, pick it up and say:

Hello!
    Moshi moshi!
    Moh-shee moh-shee!

Please get me ....
    ... wo onegai shimasu.
    ... woh oh-neh-gah'ee shee-mahss.

89

Who is speaking?
  Donata desu ka?
  Doh-nah-tah dehss kah?

This is Mr. Hayashi.
Hayashi desu.
Hah-yah-shee dehss.

Hold the wire.
  Omachi kudasai.
  Oh-mah-chee koo-dah-sah'ee.

He is not here.
  Tadaima rusu desu.
  Tah-dah'ee-mah roo-soo dehss.

Where is she?
  Kanajo wa doko e irashaimashita ka?
  Kah-nah-joh wah doh-koh eh ee-rah-shah'ee-mahsh-tah kah?

What time will he return?
  Itsu kaeri masu ka?
  It-soo kah'eh-ree mahss kah?

Will you take a message?
  Kotozute wo onegai shimasu?
  Koh-toh-zoo-teh woh oh-neh-gah'ee shee-mahss?

Tell him Mr. _____ called.
  _____ kara denwa ga atta to tsutaete kudasai.
  _____ kah-rah dehn-wah gah aht-tah toh tsoo-tah-eh-teh koo-dah-sah'ee.

Ask him to call me at _____.
  _____ ni watakushi ni denwa wo kakete kudasai to tsutaete kudasai.
  _____ nee wah-tahk-shee nee dehn-wah woh kah-keh-teh koo-dah-sah'ee toh tsoo-tah-eh-teh koo-dah-sah'ee.

I shall be here until 6.
    Watakushi wa rokuji made koko ni orimasu.
    *Wah-tahk-shee wah roh-koo-jee mah-deh koh-koh
    nee oh-ree-mahss.*

My number is Marunouchi 5511.
    Watakushi no bango wa Marunochi no go go ichi
    ichi.
    *Wah-tahk-shee noh bahn-goh wah Mah-roo-noh-
    chee noh goh goh ee-chee ee-chee.*

Thank you for your trouble.
    Oisogashii tokoro dōmo arigatō gozaimashita.
    Oh'ee-soh-gah-shee'ee toh-koh-roh DOH-*moh ah-
    ree-gah-*TOH *goh-zah'ee-mahsh-tah.*

Here are some things that may be said to you
on the telephone:

Hello!
    Moshi moshi!
    Moh-shee moh-shee!

With whom do you wish to speak?
    Donata ni ohanashi wo nasaimasu ka?
    *Doh-nah-tah nee oh-hah-nah-shee woh nah-sah'ee-
    mahss kah?*

She is out.
    Kanojō wa rusu desu.
    *Kah-noh-*JOH *wah roo-soo dehss.*

She left no message.
    Kanojō wa betsu ni kototute wo oite ikimasen
    deshita.
    *Kah-noh-*JOH *wah beht-soo nee koh-toh-too-teh
    woh oh'ee-teh ee-kee-mah-sehn dehsh-tah.*

He will be back at 6:00.

Kare wa roku ji ni kaette kimasu.

Kah-reh wah roh-koo jee nee kah-eht-teh kee-mahss.

I will give him your message.

Kare ni okotozute wo otsutae shimasu.

Kah-reh nee oh-koh-toh-zoo-teh woh oht-soo-tah'eh shee-mahss.

You have the wrong number.

Denwa bangō ga chigatte orimasu.

Dehn-wah bahn-GOH gah chee-gaht-teh oh-ree-mahss.

Nobody by that name lives here.

Sōyū kata wa kochira ni sunde orimasen.

SOH-YOO kah-tah wah koh-chee-rah nee soon-deh oh-ree-mah-sehn.

You can reach her at this number.

Kanojo ni renraku suru ni wa kono bangō e kakete kudasai.

Kah-noh-joh nee rehn-rah-koo soo-roo nee wah koh-noh bahn-GOH eh kah-keh-teh koo-dah-sah'ee.

He is away in the country.

Kare wa inaka e itte orimasu.

Kah-reh wah ee-nah-kah eh it-teh oh-ree-mahss.

XV

IF YOU WRITE OR CABLE

What's the regular postage to America?
  Amerika made no futsūbin wa ikura desu ka?
  *Ah-meh-ree-kah mah-deh noh foot-soo-been wah
  ee-koo-rah dehss kah?*

What is the airmail postage to America?
  Amerika made no kōkūbin wa ikura desu ka?
  *Ah-meh-ree-kah mah-deh noh кон-коо-been wah
  ee-koo-rah dehss kah?*

Please give me seven 100 yen stamps,
  Hyaku yen kitte no nana mai to,
  H'yah-koo yehn kit-teh noh nah-nah mah'ee toh,

  and ten 50 yen stamps.
    gojū yen kitte wo jummai kudasai.
    *goh-joo yehn kit-teh woh joo-mah'ee koo-dah-
    sah'ee.*

What's the local postage here?

Kokunai no yūbin ryōkin wa ikura desu ka?

Koh-koo-nah'ee noh YOO-*bin r'*YOH-*kin wah ee-koo-rah dehss kah?*

What's the postage for post-cards?

Hagaki no yūbin ryōkin wa ikura desu ka?

Hah-gah-kee noh YOO-*bin r'*YOH-*kin wah ee-koo-rah dehss kah?*

How much does a registered letter cost?

Kakitome yūbin wa ikura desu ka?

Kah-kee-toh-meh YOO-*bin wah ee-koo-rah dehss kah?*

Here is my address.

Watakushi no jūsho desu.

Wah-tahk-shee noh JOO-*shoh dehss.*

Where is the cable office?

Denpōkyoku wa doko desu ka?

*Den-*POH-*k'yoh-koo wah doh-koh dehss kah?*

How much does it cost by the word?

Ichi go tsuki ikura desu ka?

Ee-chee goh tsoo-kee ee-koo-rah dehss kah?

Here is the message.

Denbun wa konoyō ni onegai shimasu.

*Den-boon wah koh-noh-*YOH *nee oh-neh-gah'ee shee-mahss.*

I want to send this package.

Kono konimotsu wo hassō shitai no desu.

*Koh-noh koh-nee-moht-soo woh hahs-*SOH *shee-tah'ee noh dehss.*

I want it insured.
   Hoken wo kaketai no desu.
   Hoh-kehn woh kah-keh-tah'ee noh dehss.

In the post office they may say to you:

Where do you want to send it?
   Doko e okuri ni narimasu ka?
   Doh-koh eh oh-koo-ree nee nah-ree-mahss kah?

Air mail is 80 yen per 10 grams.
   Kōkūbin wa jū guramu ni tsuki hachijū yen desu.
   Koн-koo-bin wah joo goo-rah-moo nee tsoo-kee hah-chee-joo yehn dehss.

Do you want it insured?
   Hoken wo kakemasu ka?
   Hoh-kehn woh kah-keh-mahss kah?

Do you want it registered?
   Kakitome ni shimashu ka?
   Kah-kee-toh-mee nee shee-mahsh kah?

You must pay the tax.
   Zeikin wo harawanakereba narimasen.
   *Zeh'ee-kin woh hah-rah-wah-nah-keh-reh-bah
   nah-ree-mah-sehn.*

Write your address here.
   Koko ni anata no gojūsho wo kaite kudasai.
   *Koh-koh nee ah-nah-tah noh goh-joo-shoh woh
   kah'ee-teh koo-dah-sah'ee.*

XVI

MONEY! MONEY! MONEY!

As the American dollar is much sought after overseas, you had best devote special attention to this chapter to improve your financial vocabulary as well as your finances. Incidentally, the Japanese word for money, "kane," takes the honorific prefix "o" so that it is always said "okane"—"honorable money"—a concept not necessarily limited to Japan.

Where can I change American dollars?
Amerika no doru wo doko de kaerare masu ka?
Ah-meh-ree-kah noh doh-roo woh doh-koh deh kah'eh-rah-reh mahss kah?

Where is the bank?
Ginkō wa doko desu ka?
Ghin-кон wah doh-koh dehss kah?

Can I change dollars at the hotel?
Hoteru de doru wo kaerare masu ka?
Hoh-teh-roo deh doh-roo woh kah-eh-rah-reh mahss kah?

Will you accept traveler's checks?

Ryokō yō kogitte wo uketorimasu ka?

*R'yoh-*KOH *YOH koh-ghit-teh woh oo-keh-toh-ree-mahss kah?*

What is the rate for dollars?

Doru no sōba wa ikura desu ka?

Doh-roo noh SOH-*bah wah ee-koo-rah dehss kah?*

Is that the best rate?

Sore wa saijō no sōba desu ka?

*Soh-reh wah sah'ee-*JOH *noh* SOH-*bah dehss kah?*

I want to change $10.00.

Jū doru torikaete kudasai.

Joo doh-roo toh-ree-kah-eh-teh koo-dah-sah'ee.

Please change this check for $50.00.

Kono kogitte wo gojū doru torikaete kudasai.

*Koh-noh koh-ghit-teh woh goh-*JOO *doh-roo toh-ree-kah-eh-teh koo-dah-sah'ee.*

The rate is 360 to the dollar.

Kawase shoba wa ichi doru ni taishite sanbyaku gojū yen desu.

*Kah-wah-seh shoh-bah wah ee-chee doh-roo nee tah'ee-shee-teh sahn-b'yah-koo goh-*JOO *yehn dehss.*

Today's rate is 400 to the dollar.

Kyo no kawase sōba wa ichidoru ni taishite yohyaku yen desu.

K'yoh noh kah-wah-seh SOH-*bah wah ee-chee-doh-roo nee tah'ee-shee-teh yoh-h'yah-koo yehn dehss.*

Is this check made out to you?

Kono kogitte wa anata no meigi ni natte orimasu
ka?

*Koh-noh koh-ghit-teh wah ah-nah-tah noh
meh'ee-ghee nee naht-teh oh-ree-mahss kah?*

Sign here.

Koko e shomei shite kudasai.

Koh-koh eh shoh-meh'ee shee-teh koo-dah-sah'ee.

We don't accept travelers' checks.

Watakushitachi wa ryokō yō kogitte wo uketsuke-
masen.

*Wah-tahk-shee-tah-chee wah r'yoh-KOH YOH koh-
geet-teh woh oo-keht-soo-keh-mah-sehn.*

We cannot take a personal check.

Watakushitachi wa kojin no kogitte wo uketori-
masen.

*Wah-tahk-shee-tah-chee wah koh-jeen noh koh-
ghit-teh woh oo-keh-toh-ree-mah-sehn.*

XVII

IN AN EMERGENCY

We hope that you won't encounter any emergency, but in case you do . . .

Help!	**Police!**
Tasukete!	Junsasan!
Tahss-keh-teh!	*Joon-sah-sahn!*

Stop!
Tomari nasai!
Toh-mah-ree nah-sah'ee!

Look!
Goran nasai!
Goh-rahn nah-sah'ee!

Listen!	**Fire!**
Kiite kudasai!	Kaji!
Kee'ee-teh koo-dah-sah'ee!	*Kah-jee!*

Stop that man!
Ano hito wo tomete kudasai!
Ah-noh hee-toh woh toh-meh-teh koo-dah-sah'ee!

Hurry up!   **Go away!**
Haraku!   Ikinasai!
Hah-rah-koo!   *Ee-kee-nah-sah'ee!*

Come here!
Irasshai!
Ee-rahs-shah'ee!

Stop bothering me!
Jama wo shinai de kudasai!
Jah-mah woh shee-nah'ee deh koo-dah-sah'ee!

Look out!   **Come in!**
Abunai!   Ohairi nasai!
Ah-boo-nah'ee!   *Oh-hah'ee-ree nah-sah'ee!*

Get out!
De nasai!
Deh nah-sah'ee!

Call a doctor!
Isha wo yonde kudasai!
Ee-shah woh yohn-deh koo-dah-sah'ee!

There has been an accident.
Jiko ga arimashita.
Jee-koh gah ah-ree-mahsh-tah.

I am an American.
Watakushi wa Amerika-jin desu.
Wah-tahk-shee wah Ah-meh-ree-kah-jeen dehss.

Where is the American consul?

Amerika no ryōjikan wa doko desu ka?

Ah-meh-ree-kah noh r'YOH-jee-kahn wah doh-koh dehss kah?

I do not understand.

Watakushi wa wakarimasen.

Wah-tahk-shee wah wah-kah-ree-mah-sehn.

Call an ambulance!

Kyūkyū sha wo yonde kudasai!

K'YOO-k'YOO shah woh yohn-deh koo-dah-sah'ee!

Call the police!

Keisatsu wo yonde kudasai!

Keh'ee-saht-soo woh yohn-deh koo-dah-sah'ee!

I've been robbed!

Tōnan ni aimashita!

TOH-nahn nee ah'ee-mahsh-tah!

A man took my bag.

Otoko no hito ga watakushi no kaban wo tori-mashita.

Oh-toh-koh nòh hee-toh gah wah-tahk-shee noh kah-bahn woh toh-ree-mahsh-tah.

He went that way.

Kare wa achira ni ikimashita.

Kah-reh wah ah-chee-rah nee ee-kee-mahsh-tah.

There he is!

Kare wa soko ni imasu!

Kah-reh wah soh-koh nee ee-mahss!

I have lost my baggage.
Watakushi wa kaban wo nakushimashita.
Wah-tahk-shee wah kah-bahn woh nahk-shee-mahsh-tah.

I have lost my coat.
Koto wo nakushimashita.
Koh-toh woh nahk-shee-mahsh-tah.

I left it here last night.
Sakuya koko ni okimashita.
Sah-koo-yah koh-koh nee oh-kee-mahsh-tah.

I have lost my passport.
Watakushi wa ryoken wo nakushimashita.
Wah-tahk-shee wah r'yoh-kehn woh nahk-shee-mahsh-tah.

I have lost my wife!
Kanai wo tsuma miushinaimashita!
Kah-nah'ee woh tsoo-mah mee-oo-shee-nah'ee-mahsh-tah!

I have lost my husband!
Shujin wo miushinaimashita!
Shoo-jeen woh mee-oo-shee-nah'ee-mahsh-tah!

child!	dog!
kodomo!	inu!
koh-doh-moh!	*ee-noo!*

I have missed my train.
Kisha ni nori okuremashita.
Kee-shah nee noh-ree oh-koo-reh-mahsh-tah.

ship.	plane.	bus.
fune.	hikōki.	basu.
foo-neh.	*hee-ĸoн-kee.*	*bɑhss.*

My baggage is on board.
  Watakushi no kaban wa shanai ni oite arimasu.
  *Wah-tahk-shee noh kah-bahn wah shak-nah'ee
  nee oh'ee-teh ah-ree-mahss.*

And in an emergency, here are some things that
people may say to you:

What has happened?
  Dō shimashita ka?
  Doн shee-mahsh-tah kah?

Take it easy!
  Kiraku ni shite!
  Kee-rah-koo nee shee-teh!

Don't worry!
  Shimpai shinaide!
  Sheem-pah'ee shee-nah-ee-deh!

It's all right.
  Yoroshii desu.
  Yoh-roh-shee'ee dehss.

What's going on?
  Nani wo yatte imasu ka?
  Nah-nee woh yaht-teh ee-mahss kah?

Who did it?
  Dare ga shimashita ka?
  Dah-reh gah shee-mahsh-tah kah?

Where did he go?
Kare wa doko e ikimashita ka?
Kah-reh wah doh-koh eh ee-kee-mahsh-tah kah?

Is that the man?
Ano otoko no hito desu ka?
Ah-noh oh-toh-koh noh hee-toh dehss kah?

Is that the woman?
Ano onna no hito desu ka?
Ah-noh ohn-nah noh hee-toh dehss kah?

What was he like?
Dōyū kata deshita ka?
DOH-YOO kah-tah dehsh-tah kah?

Are you all right?
Daijōbu desu ka?
Dah'ee-JOH-boo dehss kah?

What is your name?
Anata no namae wa?
Ah-nah-tah noh nah-mah-eh wah?

Where do you live?
Doko e osumai desu ka?
Doh-koh eh oh-soo-mah'ee dehss kah?

What is your nationality?
Anata no kokuseki wa doko desu ka?
Ah-nah-tah noh kohk-seh-kee wah doh-koh dehss kah?

Where did you leave it?
Doko e oki wasuremashita ka?
Doh-koh eh oh-kee wah-soo-reh-mahsh-tah kah?

Is this it?
 Kore desu ka?
 Koh-reh dehss kah?

Finally, you may wish to say . . .

Thank you for your trouble.
 Gokurō sama deshita.
 Goh-koo-ROH sah-mah dehsh-tah.

Thank you for your kindness.
 Goshinsetsu ni arigatō gozaimashita.
 Goh-shin-seh-tsoo nee ah-ree-gah-TOH goh-zah'ee-mahsh-tah.

XVIII

WATCH THOSE SIGNS!

A WORD ABOUT JAPANESE WRITING

Japan possesses a beautiful and artistic picture-script which came from China in ancient times. It is composed of signs which we call ideographs, because they express complete ideas. While a detailed discussion of this means of writing is not within the scope of this Phrase Book, there are certain combinations of these ideographs that you will frequently see. It would be helpful for you to recognize some of them.

Exit
deguchi
deh-goo-chee

出口

Entrance
iriguchi
ee-ree-goo-chee

入口

No Admittance
deiriguchi
deh-ee-ree-goo-chee

出入禁止

Stop
tomare
toh-mah-reh

止れ

Danger
kekin
keh-kin

危険

Push
osu
oh-soo

押す

Pull
hiku
hee-koo

引く

Open
kaitenchū
*kah'ee-tehn-*CHOO

開店中

Closed
heiten
hey-tehn

閉店

Men's Room
danshi benjo
dahn-shee behn-joh

男子便所

Ladies' Room
joshi benjo
joh-shee behn-joh

女子便所

And as a matter of general interest the following Japanese ideographs stand for Tokyo, meaning "Eastern Capital;" Kobe, meaning "Spirit Gate;" Osaka, meaning "Great Slope;" and Yokohama, meaning "Side Beach."

Tōkyō   Kōbe   Ōsaka

東京 神戸 大阪

Yokohama

横浜

In addition to the ideographs or "Kan-Ji" (Japanese writing as it is called in Japan) there are two phonetic systems roughly corresponding to shorthand, of which the flowing Hiragana is used for Japanese words and the more angular Katakana is used for very simple signs and words of foreign origin. Here is the Katakana syllabary which corresponds roughly to an alphabet. We have written them in the pertinent groups of 5. Note that vowel sounds "a," "i," "u," "e," "o" are pronounced "ah," "ee," "oo," "eh," "oh."

The writing goes from top to bottom and from left to right, in the traditional Japanese fashion. The equivalent phonetic syllables are written directly under the symbols. Read down, starting here——→

ン	ワ	ラ	ヤ	マ	ハ	ナ	タ	サ	カ	ア
N	WA	RA	YA	MA	HA	NA	TA	SA	KA	A

イ	リ	イ	ミ	ヒ	ニ	チ	シ	キ	イ
I	RI	I	MI	HI	NI	CHI	SHI	KI	I

ウ	ル	ユ	ム	フ	ヌ	ツ	ス	ク	ウ
U	RU	YU	MU	FU	NU	TSU	SU	KU	U

エ	レ	エ	メ	ヘ	ネ	テ	セ	ケ	エ
E	RE	E	ME	HE	NE	TE	SE	KE	E

ヲ	ロ	ヨ	モ	ホ	ノ	ト	ソ	コ	オ
WO	RO	YO	MO	HO	NO	TO	SO	KO	O

On this basic 51-symbol syllabary the addition to the right of one set of quotation marks changes the "k" sound of the "ka" group to "g;" the "t" sound of the "ta" group to "d;" the "s" sound of the "sa" group to "z" and the "h" sound of the "ha" group to "b" In addition, a small circle, written to the right of the symbol, changes the "h" sound of the "ha" group to "p." This gives 25 additional sounds.

Taking appropriate syllables from this system it is possible to "spell" Japanese and foreign words. Here are some examples:

America

アメリカ

A-ME-RI-KA

California

カリフォルニヤ

KA-RI-FO-NI-A

Canada

カナダ

KA-NA-DA

Nihon
(The Japanese word for Japan)

ニホン

NI-HO-N

YOUR DICTIONARY & HOW TO USE IT

In the following pages you will find a different sort of dictionary. It has been especially compiled for a traveler in Japan; that is, for you! All the words that you may need will be found here, not in their abstract or poetic meanings, but in their immediate useful meaning for you as a traveler. By the time you could locate the correct expression for "Help, police!" in an ordinary dictionary, the hypothetical purse-snatcher would be far away.

Here are a few points that will help you in the use of this dictionary:

1. Verbs are given in two forms, the infinitive and the polite form. The infinitive form is given first (followed by its phonetic pronounciation in brackets [ ]) and the polite form, which is more used in conversation, shown within parentheses ( ). The polite form is the stem plus "masu" (pronounced *mahss*). Constructions where the infinitive is to be used ("able," "can," "cannot," "don't," etc.) are explained within the dictionary under the appropriate entry.

110

2. In the polite form—for example, "kikimasu," **I hear**—there is no difference between "I hear," "you hear," "he hears," etc. The pronoun is used only when there is a doubt about who is doing the action. There is also little differentiation between the present and the future. Example: "Ashita kikimasu," **Tomorrow I will hear.**

3. The negative is generally formed by substituting "en" for "u" at the end of the polite form of the verb. Example: "kikimasu," **I hear**; "kikimasen," **I don't hear.**

4. The past tense is formed by adding "mashita" (pronounced *mahsh-tah*) to the polite stem. Example: "Kikimashita," **I heard.** The negative past is formed by following the negative form of the verb with "deshita" (pronounced *dehsh-tah*). Example: "Kikimasen deshita," **I did not hear.**

5. You will often hear the word "deshō" after the infinitive or the suffix "mashō" added to the polite stem. This indicates conjecture or probability and more or less corresponds to the English future tense. Example: "Kiku deshō ka?" **Will he listen?**; "Kikimashō," **I will (probably) listen.**

6. To give commands, put "o" in front of the polite stem of the verb and follow the stem with "kudasai." Example: "O kiki kudasai!" **Listen!** To say **Don't listen!** you must get around it by saying "It isn't necessary to listen." In this case you use the infinitive: "Kiku hitsuyo wa ari masen." When asking to be given something, use

just "kudasai" preceded by "wo." Example: "Ocha wo kudasai." **Please give me tea.**

7. In making sentences note the use of the following small single-syllable words: "ga" or "wa" indicate the subject, "no" the possessive, "wo" the direct object, and "ni" or "de" location. Example: **I see Mr. Kato's cigarettes on the table.** "Watakushi wa kato-san no shigaretto wo teburu de mimasu." This is how it breaks down: I (subject) Kato-honorable's (possessive) cigarettes (object) table on (location) see (verb). Note also the fact that Japanese always places the verb at the end of the sentence.

8. Japanese nouns do not form the plural. Example: "tomodachi," **A friend;** "takusan no tomodachi," **many friends.**

9. Japanese has a talking question mark. To ask questions add "ka" to the end of the polite form of the verb: "Wakarimasu ka (?)" **Do you understand?**

(to be) **able,** dekiru [*deh-kee-roo*] (dekimasu)

NOTE: "Dekimasu" is used with "koto ga" and the infinitive of the other verb. **I am able to sing** —"Utan koto ga dekimasu."

all aboard! Minasan onori kudasai! [*Mee-nah-sahn oh-noh-ree koo-dah-sah'ee!*]
about, oyoso [*oh-yoh-soh*]
above, ue ni [*weh nee*]
abroad, kaigai e [*kah'ee-gah'ee eh*]
absent, rusu [*roohs*]

absolutely, zettai ni [*zeht-tah'ee nee*]

academy, gakuen [*gah-kwehn*]

accelerator, akuseru [*ah-koo-seh-roo*]

accident, jiko· [*jee-koh*]

account, kanjō [*kan-*JOH]

(to) **ache,** itamu [*ee-tah-moo*] (itamimasu)

acquaintance, shiriai [*shee-ree-ah'ee*]

across, mukōgawa ni [*moo-*KOH-*gah-wah nee*]

act, kōi [KOH'*ee*]

(to) **act,** enjiru [*ehn-jee-roo*] (enjimasu)

active, katsudōteki na [*kaht-soo-*DOH-*teh-kee nah*]

actor, haiyū [*hah'ee-*YOO]

actress, joyū [*joh-*YOO]

(to) **add,** tasu [*tahss*] (tashimasu)

address, jūsho [JOO-*shoh*]

addressee, jushin nin [*joo-sheen neen*]

adhesive tape, nori tsuki tēpu [*noh-ree t'soo-kee ⌐EH-poo*]

admiration, kantan [*kahn-tan*]

(to) **admire,** kanshin suru [*kahn-sheen soo-roo*] (kanshin shimasu)

admirer, keifuku sha [*keh'ee-foo-koo shah*]

(to) **admit,** ireru [*ee-reh-roo*] (iremasu)

adorable, kawairashii [*kah-wah'ee-rah-shee'ee*]

(in) **advance,** sono mae ni [*soh-noh mah-eh nee*]

advertisement, kōkoku [KOH-*koh-koo*]

advice, chūkoku [CHOO-*koh-koo*]

(to be) **afraid,** kowagaru [*koh-wah-gah-roo*] (kowagarimasu)

after, ato ni [*ah-toh nee*]

again, mata [*mah-tah*]

against, ni taishite [*nee tah'eesh-teh*]

age, toshi [*toh-shee*]

agent, dairisha [*dah'ee-ree-shah*]

ago, mae ni [*mah-eh nee*]
  two days ago, futsuka maeni [*foot-soo-kah mah-eh-nee*]
  how long ago? dono kurai mae ni? [*doh-noh koo-rah'ee mah-eh nee?*]
(to) agree, dōi suru [DOH*'ee soo-roo*] (dōi shimasu)
air, kūki [KOO-*kee*]
air force, kūgun [KOO-*goon*]
airplane, hikōki [*hee-*KOH-*kee*]
airport, kūkō [KOO-KOH]
alarm, odoroki [*oh-doh-roh-kee*]
alarm clock, mezamashi dokei [*meh-zah-mah-shee doh-keh'ee*]
alcohol, arukōru [*ah-roo-*KOH-*roo*]
all, subete [*soo-beh-teh*]
after all, tsumari [*t'soo-mah-ree*]
(to) allow, yurusu [*yoo-rooss*] (yurishimasu)
almost, hotondo [*hoh-ton-doh*]
alone, hitori de [*hee-toh-ree deh*]
along, no doko ka [*noh doh-koh kah*]
also, mo mata [*moh mah-tah*]
altar, saidan [*sah'ee-dan*]
although, no ni [*noh nee*]
ambassador, taishi [*tah'ee-shee*]
America, Amerika [*Ah-meh-ree-kah*]
American (person), Amerika-jin [*Ah-meh-ree-kah-jeen*]
ancestor, senzo [*sehn-zoh*]
ancient, mukashi no [*moo-kah-shee noh*]
and, to [*toh*]
angel, tenshi [*tehn-shee*]
anger, ikari [*ee-kah-ree*]
angry, okotta [*oh-koht-tah*]
animal, dōbutsu [DOH-*boot-soo*]
ankle, ashikubi [*ah-shee-koo-bee*]

(to) **annoy,** ira ira saseru [*ee-rah ee-rah seh-seh-roo*] (ira ira sasemasu)

answer, henji [*hehn-jee*]

antique, jidai-mono [*jee-dah'ee-moh-noh*]

anxious, ki ni naru [*kee nee nah-roo*]

anybody, daredemo [*dah-reh-deh-moh*]

anyhow, dōshitemo [DOHSH-*teh-moh*]

anything, nandemo [*nahn-deh-moh*]

anywhere, tonikaku [*toh-nee-kah-koo*]

apartment, apāto [*ah-*PAH-*toh*]

apology, benkai [*behn-kah'ee*]

(to) **appear,** arawareru [*ah-rah-wah-reh-roo*] (arawaremasu)

appetite, shokuyoku [*shoh-koo-yoh-koo*]

appetizer, apetaizā [*ah-peh-tah'ee-*ZAH]

apple, ringo [*reen-goh*]

(to) **appreciate,** kansha suru [*kan-shah soo-roo*] (kansha shimasu)

appropriate, tekitō [*teh-kee-*TOH]

(to) **approve,** mitomeru [*mee-toh-meh-roo*] (mitomemasu)

approximately, daitai [*dah'ee-tah'ee*]

Arabia, Arabiya [*Ah-rah-bee-yah*]

  Arab (person), Arabiya-jin [*Ah-rah-bee-yah-jin*]

  Arabic (language), Arabiya-go [*Ah-rah-bee-yah-goh*]

arc, yumi gata [*yoo-mee gah-tah*]

arcade, shotengai [*shoh-tehn-gah'ee*]

archbishop, dai shikyo [*dah'ee shee-k'yoh*]

architect, kenchiku [*kehn-chee-koo*]

area, menseki [*mehn-seh-kee*]

Argentina, Arujenchin [*Ah-roo-jehn-cheen*]

(to) **argue,** giron suru [*ghee-ron soo-roo*] (giron shimasu)

arm, ude [*oo-deh*]

army, rikugun [*ree-koo-goon*]

around, mawari ni [*mah-wah-ree nee*]

(to) **arrest**, taiho suru [*tah'ee-hoh soo-roo*] (taiho shimasu)

arrival, tōchaku [TOH-*chah-koo*]

(to) **arrive**, tōchaku suru [TOH-*chah-koo soo-roo*] (tōchaku shimasu)

art, geijutsu [*geh'ee-joot-soo*]

article, shinamono [*shee-nah-moh-noh*]

artificial, jinkō no [*jeen-*KOH *noh*]

artist, bijutsuka [*bee-joot-soo-kah*]

as, no yō ni [*noh* YOH *nee*]

ashtray, haizara [*hah'ee-zah-rah*]

(to) **ask**, tadzuneru [*tahd-zoo-neh-roo*] (tazune-masu)

aspirin, asupirin [*ahss-poo-reen*]

assistant, joshu [*joh-shoo*]

associate, rengō saseru [*rehn-*GOH *sah-seh-roo*] (rengo sasemasu)

association, kyōkai [*k'*YOH-*kah'ee*]

(to) **assure**, hoshō suru [*hoh-*SHOH *soo-roo*] (hoshō shimasu)

asylum, shūyō-sho [SHOO-YOH-*shoh*]

at, ni [*nee*]

athletics, kyōgi [*k'*YOH-*ghee*]

Atlantic, Taiseiyō [*Tah'ee-seh'ee-*YOH]

atmosphere, kūki [KOO-*kee*]

atom, genshi [*ghehn-shee*]

attendant, susseki [*soos-seh-kee*]

attention, chūi [CHOO'*ee*]

August, Hachigatsu [*Hah-chee-gaht-soo*]

aunt, oba [*oh-bah*]

Australia, Ostorariya [*Oh-stoh-rah-ree-yah*]

Australian (person), Ostorariya-jin

Austria, Ostoriya [*Oh-stoh-ree-yah*]

Austrian (person), Ostoriya-jin
author, sakka [*sahk-kah*]
authority, keni [*keh-nee*]
available, riyō dekiru [*ree-*YOH *deh-kee-roo*]
average, heikin [*heh'ee-keen*]
(to) **avoid,** sakeru [*sah-keh-roo*] (sakemasu)
(to) **await,** matsu [*maht-soo*] (matsumasu)
(to) **awake,** me wo samasaseru [*meh woh sah-mah-sah-seh-roo*] (samasasemasu)

baby, akanbō [*ah-kan-*BOH]
bachelor, dokushin [*dohk-sheen*]
back, ushiro [*oo-shee-roh*]
bad, warui [*wah-roo'ee*]
badly, waruku [*wah-roo-koo*]
baggage, tenimotsu [*teh-nee-moht-soo*]
balcony, barukonī [*bahr-koh-*NEE]
ball, mari [*mah-ree*]
bandage, hōtai [HOH-*tah'ee*]
bandit, akkan [*ahk-kan*]
bath, furo [*foo-roh*]
bathroom, furoba [*foo-roh-bah*]
battery, denchi [*dehn-chee*]
battle, tatakai [*tah-tah-kah'ee*]
bay, wan [*wahn*]
(to) **be,**

NOTE: The polite verb form for "to be" is "masu" for a person and "arimasu" for things. This goes for all persons, and there is no difference between "am," "is" and "are."

beach, hama [*hah-mah*]
beans, mame [*mah-meh*]
beard, hige [*hee-geh*]
beautiful, utsukushii [*oot-soo-koo-shee'ee*]

beauty parlor, biyōin [*bee-*YOH*-een*]
because, naze naraba [*nah-zeh nah-rah-bah*]
(to) **become,** ni naru [*nee nah-roo*] (ni narimasu)
bed, shindai [*sheen-dah'ee*]
bedroom, shinshitsu [*sheen-sheet-soo*]
beef, gyūniku [*g'*YOO*-nee-koo*]
before, mae ni [*mah-eh nee*]
beggar, kojiki [*koh-jee-kee*]
(to) **begin,** hajimaru [*hah-jee-mah-roo*] (hajimari-masu)
behind, ushiro ni [*oo-shee-roh nee*]
Belgian (person), Beugī-jin [*Behr-*GHEE*-jeen*]
Belgium, Beugī [*Behr-*GHEE]
(to) **believe,** shinjiru [*sheen-jee-roo*] (shinjimasu)
bell, kane [*kah-neh*]
(to) **belong to,** -ni zoku suru [*-nee zoh-koo soo-roo*] (-ni zoku shimasu)
belt, bando [*bahn-doh*]
beside, no soba ni [*noh soh-bah nee*]
best, saijō no [*sah'ee-*JOH *noh*]
better, motto yoi [*moht-toh yoh'ee*]
between, aida [*ah'ee-dah*]
big, ōkii [OH*-kee'ee*]
bird, tori [*toh-ree*]
birthday, tanjōbi [*tan-*JOH*-bee*]
black, kuro [*koo-roh*]
blanket, mōfu [MOH*-foo*]
blonde, kinpatsu [*keen-paht-soo*]
blood, chi [*chee*]
blue, ao [*ah-oh*]
boarding house, geshuku-ya [*gehsh-koo-yah*]
body, karada [*kah-rah-dah*]
(to) **boil,** niru [*nee-roo*] (nimasu)
bomb, bakudan [*bah-koo-dahn*]
bone, hone [*hoh-neh*]

book, hon [*hon*]

bookstore, hon-ya [*hon-yah*]

border, kokkyō [*kohk-k'YOH*]

(was, were) **born,** umare mashita [*oo-mah-reh mahsh-tah*]

both, ryoho no [*r'yoh-hoh noh*]

bottle, bin [*been*]

bottle opener, sen nuki [*sehn noo-kee*]

bottom, soko [*soh-koh*]

box, hako [*hah-koh*]

boy, shōnen [SHOH-*nehn*]

bracelet, udewa [*oo-deh-wah*]

brake, buriki [*boo-ree-kee*]

brains, nō [NOH]

brave, yūkan na [YOO-*kahn nah*]

bread, pan [*pahn*]

(to) **break,** kowasu [*koh-wahss*] (kowashimasu)

breakfast, chōshoku [CHOH-*shoh-koo*]

breast, mune [*moo-neh*]

breath, iki [*ee-kee*]

bride, hanayome [*hah-nah-yoh-meh*]

bridge, hashi [*hah-shee*]

bright, akarui [*ah-kah-roo'ee*]

(to) **bring,** motte kuru [*moht-teh koo-roo*] (motte kimasu)

  Please bring! Motte kite kudasai! [*Moht-teh kee-teh koo-dah-sah'ee!*]

broken, kowareta [*koh-wah-reh-tah*]

brother—

  speaker's elder brother ani [*ah-nee*]

  speaker's younger brother otōto [*oh-*TOH-*toh*]

  other person's elder brother onīsan [*oh-*NEE-*sahn*]

  other person's younger brother otōtosaɪɪ [*oh-*TOH-*toh-sahn*]

brown, cha iro [*chah ee-roh*]
brush, hake [*hah-keh*]
Buddha, Hotoke [*Hoh-toh-keh*]
Buddhist, Bukkyō [*Book-k'*YOH]
(to) burn, yaku [*yah-koo*] (yakimasu)
business, jitsugyō [*jeet-soo-g'*YOH]
busy, isogashii [*ee-soh-gah-shee'ee*]
but, karedomo [*kah-reh-doh-moh*]
butter, bata [*bah-tah*]
button, botan [*boh-tahn*]
(to) buy, kau [*kah'oo*] (kaimasu)
  I want to buy, kai tai desu [*kah'ee tah'ee dehss*]
by, no soba ni [*noh soh-bah nee*]

cabaret, kyabare [*k'yah-bah-reh*]
café, kafuē [*kah-foo'*EH]
cake, nama gashi [*nah-mah gah-shee*]
(to) call, yobu [*yoh-boo*] (yobimasu)
call (telephone), kakeru [*kah-keh-roo*] (kakemasu)
camera, kamera [*kah-meh-rah*]
can (container) kan [*kahn*]
can (to be able), (see "to be able")

> NOTE: "can" and "cannot" are expressed by the infinitive of the verb followed by "koto ga dekimasu" and "koto ga dekimasen." Example: **I (he, she) can dance.** "Odoru koto ga dekimasu." **I (he, she) cannot dance.** "Odoru koto ga dekimasen."

can opener, kan kiri [*kahn kee-ree*]
Canada, Kanada [*kah-nah-dah*]
Canadian (person), Kanada-jin
canal, unga [*oon-gah*]
(to) cancel, torikesu [*toh-ree-kehss*] (torikeshi-masu)
candy, kyandē [*k'yahn-*DEH]

capital, shufu [*shoo-foo*]

car, jidōsha [*jee-*DOH-*shah*]

card, toranpu [*toh-rahn-poo*]

care, kanri [*kan-ree*]

  (to) **take care of** (a thing), kanri suru [*kan-ree-soo-roo*] (kanri shimasu)

  (to) **take care of** (a person or animal), sewa suru [*seh-wah soo-roo*] (sewa shimasu)

carpet, jutan [*joo-tan*]

(to) **carry,** hakobu [*hah-koh-boo*] (habimasu)

cash, genkin [*ghehn-keen*]

cashier, kaikeigakari [*kah'ee-keh'ee-gah-kah-ree*]

castle, shiro [*shee-roh*]

cat, neko [*neh-koh*]

cattle, ushi [*oo-shee*]

cave, horaana [*hoh-rah-ah-nah*]

ceiling, tenjo [*tehn-joh*]

cemetery, kyodo bochi [*k'yoh-doh boh-chee*]

center, chushin [*choo-sheen*]

century, seiki [*seh'ee-kee*]

certificate, shomeisho [*shoh-meh'ee-shoh*]

chain, kusari [*koo-sah-ree*]

chair, isu [*eess*]

champagne, sanpen [*san-pehn*]

(to) **change,** kaeru [*kah-eh-roo*] (kaemasu)

chapel, kyokaido [*k'yoh-kah'ee-doh*]

charming, miryoku no aru [*mee-r'yoh-koo noh ah-roo*]

chauffeur, utenshu [*oon-tehn-shoo*]

cheap, yasui [*yah-s'wee*]

check (money), kogitte [*koh-gheet-teh*]

check (baggage), hikikaeken [*hee-kee-kah-eh-kehn*]

cherry blossom, sakura no hana [*sah-koo-rah noh hah-nah*]

cherry, sakurambo [*sah-koo-rahm-boh*]
cheese, chizu [*chee-zoo*]
chest, mune [*moo-neh*]
chicken, niwatori [*nee-wah-toh-ree*]
child, kodomo [*koh-doh-moh*]
China, Shina [*Shee-nah*]
Chinese (person), Shina-jin [*Shee-nah-jeen*]
   (language), Shina-go [*Shee-nah-goh*]
chocolate, chokolēto [*cho-koh-*LEH*-toh*]
(to) chop, kizamu [*kee-zah-moo*] (kizamimasu)
Christian, Kirisutokyō shinja [*Kee-rees-toh-k'*YOH
   sheen-jah]
Christmas, kurisumasu [*krees-mahss*]
chrysanthemum, kiku [*kee-koo*]
church, kyōkai [*k'*YOH*-kah'ee*]
cigar, hamaki [*hah-mah-kee*]
cigarette, shigaretto [*shee-gah-reht-toh*]
circle, en [*ehn*]
citizen, shimin [*shee-meen*]
city, shi [*shee*]
class, kyū [*k'*YOO]
clean, kirei [*kee-reh'ee*]
(to) clean, sōji suru [SOH*-jee soo-roo*] (sōji
   shimasu)
cleaners, shōgiki [SHOH*-ghee-kee*]
clear akiraka [*ah-kee-rah-kah*]
(to) climb, noboru [*noh-boh-roo*] (noborimasu)
(to) close, shimeru [*shee-meh-roo*] (shimasu)
closet, oshiire [*oh-shee'ee-reh*]
cloth, kire [*kee-reh*]
clothes, ifuku [*ee-foo-koo*]
cloud, kumo [*koo-moh*]
club, kurabu [*koo-rah-boo*]
coast, kaigan [*kah'ee-gan*]
coat, uwagi [*oo-wah-ghee*]

coin, kōka [кон-*kah*]

cold, tsumetai [*t'soo-meh-tah'ee*]

college, daigaku [*dah'ee-gah-koo*]

color, iro [*ee-roh*]

comb, kushi [*koo-shee*]

(to) come, kiru [*kee-roo*] (kimasu)

   come here, koko e irasshai [*koh-koh eh ee-rahs-shah'ee*]

   come in, ohairi nasai [*oh-hah-'ee-ree nah-sah'ee*]

comfortable, raku na [*rah-koo nah*]

communist (party), kyosanshugi [*k'yoh-sahn-shoo-ghee*]

company (business), kaisha [*kah-'ee-shah*]

(to) compare, kuraberu [*koo-rah-beh-roo*] (kurabemasu)

comparison, hikaku [*hee-kah-koo*]

compliment, oseji [*oh-seh-jee*]

conceited, unuboreta [*oo-noo-boh-reh-tah*]

concert, ongakukai [*ohn-gah-koo-kah'ee*]

condition, jōtai [JOH-*tah'ee*]

(to) confuse, kondo suru [*kohn-doh soo-roo*] (kondo shimasu)

congratulations! omedetō! [*oh-meh-deh-*тон!]

congress, kokkai [*kohk-kah'ee*]

(to) connect, tsunagu [*tsoo-nah-goo*] (tsunagimasu)

conservative (party), hoshushugi [*hoh-shoo-shoo-ghee*]

(to) consider, kōryo suru [кон-*r'yoh soo-roo*] (kōryo shimasu)

consulate, ryōjikan [*r'*YOH-*jee-kahn*]

(to) contain, fukumu [*foo-koo-moo*] (fukumimasu)

contented, arasou [*ah-rah-soh-oo*]

continent, tairiku [*tah'ee-ree-koo*]
(to) **continue,** tsuzukeru [*t'soo-zoo-keh-roo*]
(tsuzukemasu)
convenient, benri na [*behn-ree nah*]
(to) **cook,** ryori suru [*r'yoh-ree soo-roo*] (ryori
shimasu)
copy, utsushi [*oot-soo-shee*]
(to) **copy,** utsusu [*oot-soo-soo*] (utsushimasu)
corkscrew, sen nuki [*sehn noo-kee*]
corn, tōmorokoshi [TOH-*moh-roh-koh-shee*]
corner, kado [*kah-doh*]
correct, tadashii [*tah-dah-shee'ee*]
cost, genka [*gehn-kah*]
(to) **cost,** kakaru [*kah-kah-roo*] (kakarimasu)
cotton, wata [*wah-tah*]
(to) **count,** kazoeru [*kah-zoh-eh-roo*] (kazoemasu)
country, kuni [*koo-nee*]
courage, yūki [YOO-*kee*]
court (of law), saibansho [*sah'ee-ban-shoh*]
cow, me ushi [*meh oo-shee*]
crab, kani [*kah-nee*]
crazy, kichigai [*kee-chee-gah'ee*]
(to) **cross,** wataru [*wah-tah-roo*] (watarimasu)
crowd, zattō [*zaht*-TOH]
(to) **cry,** naku [*nah-koo*] (nakimasu)
crystal, suishō [*swee*-SHOH]
cup, koppu [*kop-poo*]
curve, kārbu [KAR-*boo*]
(to) **cut,** kiru [*kee-roo*] (kirimasu)

damage, songai [*son-gah'ee*]
damp, shikki [*sheek-kee*]
dance, odori [*oh-doh-ree*]
(to) **dance,** odoru [*oh-doh-roo*] (odorimasu)

dangerous, kiken na [*kee-kehn nah*]

dark, kurai [*koo-rah'ee*]

date (of year), hi [*hee*]

date (appointment), yakusoku [*yah-koo-soh-koo*]

daughter or **young girl,** musume [*moo-soo-meh*]

  your daughter, ojō-san [*oh-*JOH*-sahn*]

  my elder daughter, ue no musume [*oo-eh noh moo-soo-meh*]

  my younger daughter, shita no musume [*shee-tah noh moo-soo-meh*]

dead, shindciru [*shin-deh'ee-roo*]

dear (expensive), takai [*tah-kah'ee*]

dear (endearment), shinai [*sheen-ah'ee*]

December, Junigatsu [*Joo-nee-gaht-soo*]

deck, dekku [*dehk-koo*]

deep, fukai [*foo-kah'ee*]

deer, shika [*shee-kah*]

(to) **delay,** okurasu [*oh-koo-rahss*] (okurasemasu)

delight, yukai [*yoo-kah'ee*]

(to) **deliver,** todokeru [*toh-doh-keh-roo*] (todokemasu)

democracy, minshusugi [*meen-shoo-soo-ghee*]

dentist, haisha [*hah'ee-shah*]

departure, shuppatsu [*shoop-paht-soo*]

(to) **deposit,** adzukeru [*ahd-zoo-keh-roo*] (adzukerimasu)

(to) **descend,** oriru [*oh-ree-roo*] (orimasu)

(to) **describe,** arawasu [*ah-rah-wahss*] (arawashimasu)

desert, sabaku [*sah-bah-koo*]

dessert, desato [*deh-*SAH*-toh*]

(to) **develop,** hattatsu saseru [*haht-taht-soo sah-seh-roo*] (hattatsu sasemasu)

diamond, daiyamondo [*dah'ee-yah-mohn-doh*]

did, did not,

The use of "did" in the past is formed by the use of the ending "mashita" taking the place of the "masu" form of the verb. Example: **I come, I am coming:** Kimasu. **I came, I did come:** Kimashita. The negative past is formed by adding "deshita" to the negative form. **I did not come:** Kimasen deshita.

different, chigai [*chee-gah'ee*]
difficult, muzukashii [*moo-zoo-kah-shee'ee*]
dining room, shokudō [*shoh-koo-*DOH]
dinner, bansan [*bahn-sahn*]
(to) **direct,** shidō suru [*shee-*DOH *soo-roo*] (shidō shimasu)
direction, hōkō [HOH-KOH]
director, torishimariyaku [*toh-ree-shee-mah-ree-yah-koo*]
dirty, yogoreta [*yoh-goh-reh-tah*]
disadvantage, fuben [*foo-behn*]
discount, waribiki [*wah-ree-bee-kee*]
dish, sara [*sah-rah*]
(to) **disinfect,** shōdoku suru [SHOH-*doh-koo soo-roo*] (shōdoku shimasu)
(to) **dismiss,** kaisan suru [*kah'ee-sahn soo-roo*] (kaisan shimasu)
distance, kyori [*k'yoh-ree*]
(to) **disturb,** jama suru [*jah-mah soo-roo*] (jama shimasu)
(to) **divorce,** rikon suru [*ree-kohn soo-roo*] (rikon shimasu)
(to) **do,** suru [*soo-roo*] (shimasu)

(For use of questions formed with **do** in English, see point 9 on page 112.)

dock, hatoba [*hah-toh-bah*]
doctor, isha [*ee-shah*]
dog, inu [*ee-noo*]
doll, ningyō [*neen-g'YOH*]
dollar, doru [*doh-roo*]
domestic, kokunai no [*koh-koo-nah'ee noh*]
done, kansei shita [*kahn-seh'ee shee-tah*]
donkey, roba [*roh-bah*]
don't, do not,

NOTE: To give negative commands as in telling somebody not to do something, it is necessary to use a polite expression such as "it is not necessary to...." To make this construction, use the infinitive form of the verb. In the following construction, **Don't do that:** Suru hitsuyo wa nai.

door, to [*toh*]
dose, ippuku [*eep-pook*]
double, nijū [*nee-*JOO]
doubtful, utagawashii [*oo-tah-gah-wah-shee'ee*]
down, shita e [*shee-tah eh*]
dozen, ichi dāsu [*ee-chee* DAH-*soo*]
dragon, ryū [*r'*YOO]
drawer, hikidashi [*hee-kee-dah-shee*]
dress, doresu [*doh-rehss*]
dress maker, doresu meikā [*doh-rehss meh-ee-*KAH]
(to) **drink,** nomu [*noh-moo*] (nomimasu)
(to) **drive,,** unten suru [*oon-tehn soo-roo*] (unten shimasu)
driver, untenshu [*oon-tehn-shoo*]

drugstore, yakkyoku [*yahk-k'yoh-koo*]
drunk, yotta [*yoht-tah*]
dry, kawaita [*kah-wah'ee-tah*]
duck, kamo [*kah-moh*]
dust, hokori [*hoh-koh-ree*]

each, meimei no [*meh'ee-meh'ee noh*]
each one, kakujin (*kah-koo-jeen*)
ear, mimi [*mee-mee*]
early, hayai [*hah-yah'ee*]
(to) **earn,** mōkeru [MOH-*keh-roo*] (mōkemasu)
earthquake, jishin [*jee-shin*]
east, higashi [*hee-gah-shee*]
easy, yasashii [*yah-sah-shee'ee*]
(to) **eat,** taberu [*tah-beh-roo*] (tabemasu)
edge, hashi [*hah-shee*]
education, kyōiku [*k'YOH'ee-koo*]
egg, tamago [*tah-mah-goh*]
Egypt, Ejiputo [*Eh-jeep-toh*]
Egyptian (person), Ejiputo-jin [*Eh-jeep-toh-jeen*]
eight, hachi [*hah-chee*]
eighteen, jūhachi [JOO-*hah-chee*]
eight hundred, happyaku [*hahp-p'yah-koo*]
eighty, hachijū [*hah-chee-*JOO]
either, dochira ka [*doh-chee-rah kah*]
elastic, danryoku no aru [*dahn-r'yoh-koo noh ah-roo*]
elbow, hiji [*hee-jee*]
electric, denki [*dehn-kee*]
elevator, erebētā [*eh-reh-*BEH-TAH]
eleven, jūichi [JOO-*ee-chee*]
(to be) **embarrassed,** komaraseru [*koh-mah-rah-seh-roo*] (komarasemasu)
(to) **embrace,** daku [*dah-koo*] (dakimasu)
embroidery, shishū [*shee-*SHOO]

emerald, emerarudo [*eh-meh-rah-roo-doh*]

emergency, kinkyū [*kin-k'*YOO]

emotion, kanjōh [*kahn-*JOH]

Emperor, Tennō [*tehn-*NOH]

Empire, Teikoku [*Teh'ee-koh-koo*]

empty, kara [*kah-rah*]

encore! ankōru! [*ahn-*KOH-*roo!*]

end, owari [*oh-wah-ree*]

(to) end, oeru [*oh-eh-roo*] (oemasu)

(to) engage, yakusoku suru (*yah-koo-soh-koo soo-roo*] (yakusoku shimasu)

engaged, yokaku zumi [*yoh-kah-koo zoo-mee*]

England, Eikoku [*Eh-koh-koo*]
  English (person), Eikoku-jin [*Eh'ee-koh-koo-jeen*]
  English (language), Eigo [*Eh'ee-go*]

enough, jūbun [JOO-*boon*]

(to) enter, hairu [*hah'ee-roo*] (hairimasu)

entertaining, yukai na [*yoo-kah'ee nah*]

enthusiastic, nekkyō-teki na [*nehk-k'*YOH-*teh-kee nah*]

entire, subete [*soo-beh-teh*]

entrance, iriguchi [*ee-ree-goo-chee*]

envelope, fūto [FOO-*toh*]

equal, dōtō no [DOH-TOH *noh*]

equator, sekidō [*seh-kee-*DOH]

equipment, setsubi [*seht-soo-bee*]

error, ayamari [*ah-yah-mah-ree*]

estate, zaisan [*zah'ee-sahn*]

Europe, Yōroppa [YOH-*rohp-pah*]
  European (person), Yōroppa-jin [YOH-*rohp-pah-jeen*]

even, doitsu no [*doh'ee-t'soo noh*]

evening, yūgata [YOO-*gah-tah*]

every, arayuru [*ah-rah-yoo-roo*]

everybody, dare demo [*dah-reh deh-moh*]
everything, nan demo [*nahn deh-moh*]
evidently, akirakani [*ah-kee-rah-kah-nee*]
exact, seikaku na [*seh'ee-kah-koo nah*]
examination (medical), kensa [*kehn-sah*]
examination (education), shiken [*shee-kehn*]
(to) **examine,** shiraberu [*shee-rah-beh-roo*]
(shirabemasu)
example, mihon [*mee-hohn*]
except, no hoka ni [*noh hoh-kah nee*]
(to) **exchange,** kōkan suru [KOH-*kahn soo-roo*]
(kōkan shimasu)
excursion, yūran [YOO-*rahn*]
Excuse me! Shitsurei shimasu! [*sheet-soo-reh'ee
shee-mahss!*] or
Gomen nasai! [*Goh-mehn nah-sah'ee!*]
exercise, renshū [*rehn-*SHOO]
exhibition, tenrankai [*ten-rahn-kah'ee*]
exit, deguchi [*deh-goo-chee*]
(to) **expect,** kitai suru [*kee-tah'ee soo-roo*] (kitai
shimasu)
expenses, hiyō [*hee-*YOH]
expensive, kōka [KOH-*kah*]
(to) **explain,** setsumei suru [*set-soo-meh'ee soo-
roo*] (setsumei shimasu)
export, yushutsu [*yoo-shoot-soo*]
(to) **export,** yushutsu suru [*yoo-shoot-soo soo-roo*]
(yushutsu shimasu)
express, kyūkō [*k'*YOO-KOH]
extra, yobun [*yoh-boon*]
extravagant, hōgai na [HOH-*gah'ee nah*]
eye, me [*meh*]

face, kao [*kah'oh*]
factory, kōba [KOH-*bah*]

(to) **fade,** aseru [*ah-seh-roo*] (asemasu)

fainting spell, memai ga suru [*meh-mah'ee gah soo-roo*]

(to) **fall,** ochiru [*oh-chee-roo*] (ochimasu)

false, fusei na [*foo-seh'ee nah*]

family, kazoku [*kah-zoh-koo*]

famous, yūmei [YOO-*meh'ee*]

fan, uchiwa [*oo-chee-wah*]

far, tooku [*toh-oh-koo*]

fare, ryōkin [*r'*YOH-*kin*]

farm, nōjō [NOH-JOH]

farmer, hyakushō [*h'yah-koo*-SHOH]

farther, motto tōku [*moht-toh* TOH-*koo*]

fashion, ryūkō [*r'*YOO-KOH]

fat, futotta [*foo-toht-tah*]

(my) **father,** chichi [*chee-chee*]
  (your) **father,** otōsan [*oh*-TOH-*sahn*]

fault, kashitsu [*kah-sheet-soo*]

favor, kōi [KOH-*ee*]

feather, hane [*hah-neh*]

February, Nigatsu [*Nee-gaht-soo*]

(to) **feel,** kanjiru (*kahn-jee-roo*) (kanjimasu)

feeling, kibun [*kee-boon*]

female, onna [*ohn-nah*]

fence, kaki [*kah-kee*]

fender, fendā [*fehn*-DAH]

few, sukoshi [*soo-koh-shee*]

fiancé(e), iinazuke [*ee'ee-nahss-keh*]

field, hara [*hah-rah*]

fifteen, jūgo [JOO-*goh*]

fifty, gojū [*goh*-JOO]

(to) **fight,** tatakau [*tah-tah-kah'oo*] (tatakimasu)

(to) **fill,** ippai ni suru [*eep-pah'ee nee soo-roo*]

filling, tsumemono [*t'soo-meh-moh-noh*]

film, fuirumu [*foo'ee-roo-moo*]
final, saishūno [*sah'ee-*SHOO*-noh*]
(to) **find,** mitsukeru [*meet-soo-keh-roo*] (mitsuke-masu)
fine (delicate), yuryōna [*yoo-r'*YOH*-nah*]
fine (well), genki [*gehn-kee*]
finger, yubi [*yoo-bee*]
(to) **finish,** sumasu [*soo-mahss*] (sumasemasu)
fire, hi [*hee*]
first, ichiban [*ee-chee-bahn*]
fish, sakana [*sah-kah-nah*]
fisherman, gyofu [*g'yoh-foo*] (ryōshi)
fishing, tsuri [*tsoo-ree*]
(to) **fit,** au [*ah'oo*] (aimasu)
five, go [*goh*]
(to) **fix,** naosu [*nah-oh-soo*] (naoshimasu)
flag, hata [*hah-tah*]
flat, taira na [*tah'ee-rah nah*]
flavor, aji [*ah-jee*]
flight, hikō [*hee-*KOH]
flood, ōmizu [OH-*mee-zoo*]
floor, uka [*oo-kah*]
flower, hana [*hah-nah*]
  flower arrangement, ikebana [*ee-keh-bah-nah*]
(to) **fly,** tobu [*toh-boo*] (tobimasu)
fly (insect), hae [*hah'eh*]
fog, kiri [*kee-ree*]
(to) **follow,** shitagau [*shee-tah-gah-oo*] (shitagai-masu)
food, tabemono [*tah-beh-moh-noh*]
foot, ashi [*ah-shee*]
for, no tame ni [*noh tah-meh nee*]
(to) **forbid,** kinjiru [*kin-jee-roo*] (kinjimasu)
foreign, gaikoku [*gah'ee-koh-koo*]
foreigner, gaikoku-jin [*gah'ee-koh-koo-jeen*]

forest, hayashi [*hah-yah-shee*]

(to) **forgive,** yurusu [*yoo-roo-soo*] (yuru shimasu)

fork, fōku [FOH-*koo*]

form, katachi [*kah-tah-chee*]

formal, seishiki no [*seh'ee-shee-kee noh*]

former, mae no [*mah-eh noh*]

fort, toride [*toh-ree-deh*]

fortunate, shiawase na [*shee-ah-wah-seh nah*]

fortunately, kōun ni [KOH-*oon nee*]

fortune, un [*oon*] or shiju [*shee-joo*]

forty, yonju [*yohn-joo*]

forward, mae ni [*mah-eh nee*]

fountain, funsui [*foon-swee*]

fountain pen, mannenhitsu [*mahn-nehn-hit-soo*]

four, yon [*yohn*] or shi [*shee*]

fox, kitsune [*kit-soo-neh*]

fragile, kowareyasui [*koh-wah-reh-yah-swee*]

France, Furansu [*Frahnss*]

free, tada no [*tah-dah noh*]

freedom, jiyū [*jee-*YOO]

freight, kamotsu [*kah-moht-soo*]

French (language), Furansu-go [*Frahnss-goh*]

French (person), Furansu-jin [*Frahnss-jeen*]

frequently, shiba shiba [*shee-bah shee-bah*]

fresh, shinsen na [*sheen-sehn nah*]

Friday, Kinyōbi [*Kin-*YOH-*bee*]

fried, furai [*foo-rah'ee*]

friend, tomodachi [*toh-moh-dah-chee*]

frog, kaeru [*kah-eh-roo*]

from, kara [*kah-rah*]

front, mae [*mah-eh*]

frozen, kōtta [KOHT-*tah*]

fruit, kudamono [*koo-dah-moh-noh*]

full, ippai [*ip-pah'ee*]

funeral, osōshiki [*oh-*SOH-*shee-kee*]

funny, okashii [*oh-kah-shee'ee*]
fur, kegawa [*keh-gah-wah*]
furniture, kagu [*kah-goo*]
further, sono ue no [*soh-noh oo'eh noh*]
future, shōrai [SHOH-*rah'ee*]

gallon, garon [*gah-rohn*]
gambling, tobaku [*toh-bah-koo*]
game, asobi [*ah-soh-bee*]
garage, garēji [*gah-*REH-*jee*]
garbage, gomi [*goh-mee*]
garden, niwa [*nee-wah*]
garlic, ninniku [*neen-nee-koo*]
gasoline, gasorin [*gah-soh-reen*]
gate, mon [*mohn*]
gay, yōki na [YOH-*kee nah*]
gear (car), giya [*ghee-yah*]
general, ippan no [*ip-pahn noh*]
generally, ippan ni [*ip-pahn nee*]
generous, kandai na [*kahn-dah'ee nah*]
gentleman, shinshi [*sheen-shee*]
geography, chiri [*chee-ree*]
German (person), Doitsu-jin [*Doyt-soo-jeen*]
German (language), Doitsu-go [*Doyt-soo-goh*]
Germany, Doitsu [*Doyt-soo*]
(to) **get,** morau [*moh-rah-oo*] (moraimasu)
  (to) **get down,** oriru [*oh-ree-roo*] (orimasu)
  (to) **get married,** kekkon suru [*kehk-kohn soo-roo*] (kekkon shimasu)
  (to) **get off,** oriru [*oh-ree-roo*] (orimasu)
  (to) **get up,** okiru [*oh-kee-roo*] (okimasu)
ghost, obake [*oh-bah-keh*]
gift, okurimono [*oh-koo-ree-moh-noh*]
gin, gin [*jeen*]
girl, musume [*moo-soo-meh*]

(to) **give,** (speaker is giving to other person) ageru [*ahg-eh-roo*] (agemasu)

(to) **give** (other person is giving to speaker), kureru [*koo-reh-roo*] (kudasaimasu)

NOTE: The reason there are two forms of "to give" is another instance of Japanese politeness. When the speaker gives he is giving *up* to the other person, while the person spoken to is giving *down* to the speaker.

give me, —watakushi ni kudasai [*wah-tahk-shee nee koo-dah-sah'ee*]

glad, yorokonde [*yoh-roh-kohn-deh*]

glass, garasu [*gah-rahss*]

glasses (eye), megane [*meh-gah-neh*]

glove, tebukuro [*teh-boo-koo-roh*]

glue, nikawa [*nee-kah-wah*]

(to) **go,** iku [*ee-koo*] (ikimasu)

(to) **go away,** saru [*sah-roo*] (sarimasu)

Let's go! Ikimasho! [*Ee-kee-mah-shoh!*]

(to) **go back,** kaeru [*kah-eh-roo*] (kaerimasu)

(to) **go in,** hairu [*hah'ee-roo*] (hairimasu)

(to) **go out,** deru [*deh-roo*] (demasu)

(to) **go to bed,** neru [*neh-roo*] (nemasu)

god, kami sama [*kah-mee sah-mah*]

gold, kin [*kin*]

golf, gorufu [*goh-roo-foo*]

good, ii [*ee-ee*] or yoi [*yoh'ee*]

goodbye, sayōnara [*sah-YOH-nah-rah*]

good-looking, kiryō no yoi [*kee-r'YOH noh yoh'ee*]

gossip, uwasa [*oo-wah-sah*]

government, seifu [*seh'ee-foo*]

(to) **graduate,** sotsugyō suru [*soht-soo-g'YOH soo-roo*] (sotsugyō shimasu)

grandson, mago [*mah-goh*]

granddaughter, mago musume [*mah-goh moo-soo-meh*]

grandfather, ojiisan [*oh-jee'ee-sahn*]

grandmother, obaasan [*oh-bah'ah-sahn*]

grape, budō [*boo-*DOH]

grapefruit, gureipu furūtsu [*greh'ee-poo foo-*ROOT-*soo*]

grass, kusa [*koo-sah*]

grateful, arigataku omou [*ah-ree-gah-tah-koo oh-moh-oo*]

gravy, gurebi [*goo-reh-bee*]

gray, haiiro [*hah-ee'ee-roh*]

grease, abura [*ah-boo-rah*]

great, idai na [*ee-dah'ee nah*]

Greece, Girisha [*Gree-shah*]

Greek (person), Girisha-jin [*Gree-shah-jeen*]

Greek (language), Girisha-go [*Gree-shah-goh*]

green, aoi [*ah-oh'ee*]

groceries, shokuryo zakka [*shoh-koo-r'yoh zahk-kah*]

ground, jimen [*jee-mehn*]

(to) **grow** (for people or animals), seichō suru [*seh'ee-*CHOH *soo-roo*] (seicho shimasu)

(to) **grow** (crops), saibai suru [*sah'ee-bah'ee soo-roo*] (saibai shimasu)

(to) **guarantee,** hosho suru [*hoh-shoh soo-roo*] (hosho shimasu)

guest, okyaku [*oh-k'yah-koo*]

guide, annaisha [*ahn-nah'ee-shah*]

gum (chewing), chūin gamu [*CHOO-ehn gah-moo*]

gun, jū [JOO]
gymnasium, taiiku-kan [*tah'ee-ee-koo-kahn*]

(to) **have,** motte iru [*moht-teh ee-roo*] (motte imasu)

> NOTE: To say "have you?" use "arimasu ka" preceded by "ga." "Have you a cigarette?"—"Shigaretto ga arimasu ka?"

(to) **have to,** See *must*
Hawaii, Hawaii [*Hah-wah-ee'ee*]
he, kare [*kah-reh*]
head, atama [*ah-tah-mah*]
headache, zutsū [*zoot-*SOO]
(to) **heal,** naosu [*nah-oh-soo*] (naoshimasu)
healthy, kenkō na [*kehn-*KOH *nah*]
  (to your) **health!** Gokenkō wo shuku shimasu! [*Goh-kehn-*KOH *woh shoo-koo shee-mahss!*]
(to) **hear,** kiku [*kee-koo*] (kikimasu)
heart, shinzō [*sheen-*ZOH]
heat, atsusa [*aht-soo-sah*]
heaven, tengoku [*tehn-goh-koo*]
heel, kakato [*kah-kah-toh*]
hell, gigoku [*gee-goh-koo*]
hello (on phone), moshi moshi [*moh-shee moh-shee*]
(to) **help,** tasukeru [*tahss-keh-roo*] (tasukemasu)
help! tasukete! [*tah-soo-keh-teh!*]
helpful, yaku ni tatsu [*yah-koo nee taht-soo*]
hen, men dori [*mehn doh-ree*]
her, kanojo [*kah-noh-joh*]
here, koko [*koh-koh*]
high, takai [*tah-kah'ee*]
hill, oka [*oh-kah*]
(to) **him,** kare ni [*kah-reh nee*]

him, kare wo [*kah-reh woh*]

(to) **hire,** yatou [*yah-toh'oo*] (yatoimasu)

his, kare no [*kah-reh noh*]

historical, rekishi jo no [*reh-kee-shee joh noh*]

history, rekishi [*reh-kee-shee*]

(to) **hit,** utsu [*oot-soo*] (uchimasu)

(to) **hold,** daku [*dah-koo*] (dakimasu)

hole, ana [*ah-nah*]

holding, shoyū [*shoh-*YOO]

holiday, saijitsu [*sah'ee-jeet-soo*]

holy, shinsei na [*sheen-seh'ee nah*]

home, uchi [*oo-chee*]

honest, shōjiki [SHOH-*jee-kee*]

honey, mitsu [*meet-soo*]

honeymoon, shin kon ryokō [*sheen kon r'yoh-*KOH]

honor, meiyo [*meh'ee-yoh*]

hook, kagi [*kah-ghee*]

hope, nozomi [*noh-zoh-mee*]

(to) **hope,** nozomu [*noh-zoh-moo*] (nozomimasu)

horn, tsuno [*t'soo-noh*]

horse, uma [*oo-mah*]

horseback, ùma nori [*oo-mah noh-ree*]

hospital, byōin [*b'*YOH-*een*]

hostess, hosutesu [*hoss-tess*]

hot, atsui [*aht-swee*]

hotel, hoteru (generally refers to western-style) [*hoh-teh-roo*]

    ryokan (Japanese-style) [*r'yoh-kahn*]

hour, jikan [*jee-kahn*]

house, uchi [*oo-chee*]

how, dō [DOH]

  how far? dono kurai arimasu ka? [*doh-noh koo-rah'ee ah-ree-mahss kah?*]

  how long? (time), dono kurai? [*doh-noh koo-rah'ee?*]

how many? dorehodo? [*doh-reh-hoh-doh?*]

how much? ikahodo desu ka? [*ee-kah-hoh-doh dehss kah?*]

however, ikani . . . demo [*ee-kah-nee . . . deh-moh*]

hundred, hyaku [*h'yah-koo*]

Hungarian (language), Hangariya-go [*Hahn-gah-ree-yah-goh*]

   Hungarian (person), Hangariya-jin [*Hahn-gah ree-yah-jeen*]

Hungary, Hangariya [*Hahn-gah-ree-yah*]

hunger, kūfuku [KOO-*foo-koo*]

hungry, tabetai [*tah-beh-tah'ee*]

hunting, kari [*kah-ree*]

hurricane, bofu [*boh-foo*]

Hurrah! Banzai! [*Bahn-zah'ee*] literally "10,000 years!"

hurry, isogi [*ee-soh-ghee*]

hurrying, isoide [*ee-soh'ee-deh*]

(It) hurts! Itai! [*Ee-tah'ee!*]

husband, otto [*oht-toh*]

   (my) **husband,** shujin [*shoo-jin*]

   (your) **husband,** go shujin [*goh shoo-jin*]

I, watakushi [*wah-tahk-shee*]

ice, kōri [KOH-*ree*]

icecream, aisukurīmu [*ah-ees-*KREEM]

idea, kangae [*kahn-gah-eh*]

ideal, risōteki na [*ree-*SOH*-teh-kee nah*]

identical, dōitsu no [DOH-*eet-soo noh*]

identity, mimoto [*mee-moh-toh*]

idiot, hakuchi [*hah-koo-chee*]

idle, namakemono [*nah-mah-keh-moh-noh*]

if, moshi . . . naraba [*moh-shee . . . nah-rah-bah*] "moshi" comes before the verb, "naraba" follows the verb.)

ignorant, muchi na [*moo-chee nah*]
ill, byōki no [*b'*YOH*-kee noh*]
illegal, fuhō na [*foo-*HOH *nah*]
illustration, kaisetsu [*kah'ee-seht-soo*]
imagination, kūsō [KOO-SOH]
imitation, mane [*mah-neh*]
immediate, sokuza no [*soh-koo-zah noh*]
impossible, fukanō [*foo-kah-*NOH]
important, jūyō [JOO-YOH]
imported, yunyū suru [*yoon-*YOO *soo-roo*]
importer, yunyu gyōsha [*yoon-yoo g'*YOH*-shah*]
(to) **improve,** kairyō suru [*kah-ee-r'*YOH *soo-roo*]
    (kairyō shimasu)
in, no naka ni [*noh nah-kah nee*]
inch,

NOTE: The Japanese do not use inches but centi-
meters. A centimeter (*senchimetoru*) is approximately ⅖ of an inch.

incident, dekigoto [*deh-kee-goh-toh*]
included, fukumu [*foo-koo-moo*]
income, shotoku [*shoh-toh-koo*]
incomplete, fukanzen na [*foo-kahn-zehn nah*]
inconvenience, fuben [*foo-behn*]
incredible, shinyō dekinai [*shin-*YOH *deh-kee-*
    nah-ee]
indeed, hontō ni [*hohn-*TOH *nee*]
indefinite, mugen no [*moo-ghehn noh*]
independence, dokuritsu [*doh-koo-reet-soo*]
independent, dokuritsu shita [*doh-koo-reet-soo*
    shee-tah]
India, Indo [*In-doh*]
Indian (person), Indo-jin
indigestion, fushōka [*foo-*SHOH*-kah*]

individually, betsu-betsu ni [*beht-soo beht-soo nee*]

Indonesia, Indonesiya [*In-doh-neh-see-yah*]

Indonesian (person), Indonesia-jin

Indonesian (language), Indonesia-go

indoor, uchi ni [*oo-chee nee*]

industrial, sangyō no [*sahn-g'YOH noh*]

infant, yōji [YOH-*jee*]

infection, densen [*dehn-sehn*]

infectious, densen suru [*dehn-sehn soo-roo*]

informal, ryakushiki no [*r'yah-koo-shee-kee noh*]

inhabitant, jūmin [JOO-*min*]

injection, chūsha [CHOO-*shah*]

injury, kega [*keh-gah*]

ink, inku [*een-koo*]

inn, ryokan [*r'yoh-kahn*]

innocent, muzai no [*moo-zah'ee noh*]

(to) **inquire,** tazuneru [*tah-zoo-neh-roo*] (tazune-masu)

insane, kichigai no [*kee-chee-gah'ee noh*]

insect, mushi [*moo-shee*]

(to) **insist,** iiharu [*ee'ee-hah-roo*] (iiharimasu)

(to) **inspect,** kensa suru [*kehn-sah soo-roo*] (kensa shimasu)

instead, kawari ni [*kah-wah-ree nee*]

institution, gakkukō [*gahk-koo-*KOH]

instructor, kyōsi [*k'*YOH-*see*]

insurance, hoken [*hoh-kehn*]

(to) **insure,** kakuho suru [*kah-koo-hoh soo-roo*] (kakuho shimasu)

intact, moto no mama no [*moh-toh noh mah-mah noh*]

intelligent, kyōyō no aru [*k'*YOH-YOH *noh ah-roo*]

intense, hageshii [*hah-geh-shee'ee*]

intention, mokuteki [*moh-koo-teh-kee*]

interesting, omoshiroi [*oh-moh-shee-roh'ee*]
interior, naibu no [*nah'ee-boo noh*]
intermission, naka yasumi [*nah-kah yahss-mee*]
internal, naimenteki [*nah'ee-mehn-teh-kee*]
international, kokusai [*koh-koo-sah'ee*]
(to) **interpret,** ... wo setsumei suru [*woh seht-soo-meh'ee soo-roo*] (wo setsumei shimasu)
interpreter, tsūyaku [TSOO-*yah-koo*]
interview, menkai [*mehn-kah'ee*]
into, no naka e [*noh nah-kah eh*]
(to) **introduce,** shōkai suru [SHOH-*kah'ee soo-roo*) (shōkai shimasu)
invention, hatsumei [*haht-soo-meh'ee*]
(to) **invite,** shōtai suru [SHOH-*tah'ee soo-roo*] (shōtai shimasu)
iodine, yōdochinki [YOH-*doh-chin-kee*]
Ireland, Airulando [*Ah-eer-lahn-doh*]
Irish (person), Airulando-jin
iron, tetsu [*teht-soo*]
(to) **iron,** airon wo kakeru [*ah-ee-rohn woh kah-keh-roo*] (airon wo kakemasu)
Isn't it so? So desu ne? [*Soh dehss neh?*]
island, shima [*shee-mah*]
Israel, Isuraeru [*Ees-rah-eh-roo*]
Israeli, Isuraeru-jin [*Ees-rah-eh-roo-jeen*]
it (It does not exist in Japanese; use pronouns **this** or **that** "kore" or "sore.")
Italian (language), Itarī-go [*Ee-tah-*REE-*goh*]
Italian (person), Itarī-jin [*Ee-tah-*REE-*jeen*]
Italy, Itarī [*Ee-tah-*REE]
(to) **itch,** kayuku naru [*kah-yoo-koo nah-roo*]
ivory, zōge [ZOH-*geh*]

jade, hisui [*hee-swee*]
jail, rōgoku [ROH-*goh-koo*]

January, Ichigatsu [*Ee-chee-gaht-soo*]

Japan, Nihon [*Nee-hohn*]

Japanese (language), Nihon-go [*-goh*]

Japanese (person), Nihon-jin [*-jeen*]

Japanese (bath), Nihon furo [*foo-roh*]

Japanese (inn), Nihon yadoya [*yah-doh-yah*]

Japanese (restaurant), Nihon riyori ya [*ree-yoh-ree yah*]

Jewish (person), Yudaya-jin [*Yoo-dah-yah-jeen*]

job, shigoto [*shee-goh-toh*]

joke, jōdan [JOH-*dahn*]

judge, saibankan [*sah'ee-bahn-kahn*]

juice, jūsu [JOO-*soo*]

July, Hichigatsu [*Hee-chee-gaht-soo*]

(to) jump, tobu [*toh-boo*] (tobimasu)

June, Rokugatsu [*Roh-koo-gaht-soo*]

jungle, mitsurin [*meet-soo-reen*]

just (now), tatta ima [*taht-tah ee-mah*]

just (only), tan ni [*tahn nee*]

justice, seigi [*seh'ee-ghee*]

(to) keep, motte iru [*moht-teh ee-roo*] (motte imasu)

kerosene, tōyu [TOH-*yoo*]

key, kagi [*kah-ghee*]

keyboard, kenban [*kehn-bahn*]

kid, koyagi [*koh-yah-ghee*]

kidney, jinzō [*jeen-*ZOH]

(to) kill, korosu [*koh-roh-soo*] (koroshimasu)

kilometer, kiromētoru [*kee-roh-*MEH-*toh-roo*]; approximately ⅝ of a mile.

kind, shurui [*shoo-roo'ee*]

kindly, shinsetsu na [*shin-set-soo nah*]

king, ōsama [OH-*sah-mah*]

kiss, seppun [*sehp-poon*]

kitchen, daidokoro [*dah'ee-doh-koh-roh*]
kleenex tissues, chirigami [*chee-ree-gah-mee*]
knee, hiza [*hee-zah*]
knife, hōchō [HOH-CHOH]
knight, kishi [*kee-shee*]
(to) knock, tataku [*tah-tah-koo*] (tatakimasu)
(to) know, shiru [*shee-roo*] (shirimasu)
Korea, Chōsen [CHOH-*sehn*]
Korean (language), Chōsen-go [*-goh*]
Korean (person), Chōsen-jin [*-jeen*]

laborer, rōdōsha [ROH-DOH-*shah*]
lady, fujin [*foo-jeen*]
  ladies' room, onna no gofujō [*ohn-nah noh goh-foo-*JOH]
lake, mizuuni [*mee-zoo-oo-nee*]
lamb, kohitsuji [*koh-hit-soo-jee*]
lamp, rampu [*rahm-poo*]
land, riku [*ree-koo*]
landlady, onna yanushi [*ohn-nah yah-noo-shee*]
landlord, yanushi [*yah-noo-shee*]
lane, roji [*roh-jee*]
language, kotoba [*koh-toh-bah*]
lantern, chōchin [CHOH-*chin*]
large, ōkii [OH-*kee'ee*]
last, saigo no [*sah'ee-goh noh*]
late, osoi [*oh-soh'ee*]
later, ato de [*ah-toh deh*]
(to) laugh, warau [*wah-rah'oo*] (waraimasu)
laundress, sentaku onna [*sehn-tah-koo ohn-nah*]
laundry, sentaku-ya [*sehn-tah-koo-yah*]
lavatory, tearaijo [*teh-ah-rah'ee-joh*]
law, hōritsu [HOH-*reet-soo*]
lawyer, bengoshi [*behn-goh-shee*]

lazy, namakemono [*nah-mah-keh-moh-noñ*]
leader, shidōsha [*shee-*DOH*-shah*]
leaf, ha [*hah*]
leak, moru [*moh-roo*]
(to) **learn,** narau [*nah-rah'oo*] (narimasu)
least, saishō no [*sah'ee-*SHOH *noh*]
leather, kawa [*kah-wah*]
(to) **leave,** saru [*sah-roo*] (sarimasu)
lecture, kōgi [KOH*-ghee*]
left, hidari [*hee-dah-ree*]
leg, ashi [*ah-shee*]
lemon, remon [*reh-mohn*]
lemonade, remonēdo [*reh-moh-*NEH*-doh*]
(to) **lend,** kasu [*kah-soo*] (kashimasu)
less, yori sukunai [*yoh-ree soo-koo-nah'ee*]
(to) **let** (permit), saseru [*sah-seh-roo*] (sashimasu)
   let's: This concept is expressed by "masho"
      added to the polite stem of the verb: "Sari-
      masho!" **Let's leave!**
letter, tegami [*teh-gah-mee*]
lettuce, retasu [*reh-tahss*]
level, suijun [*swee-joon*]
liberty, jiyū [*jee-*YOO]
license, menkyo [*mehn-k'yoh*]
lie (untruth), uso [*oo-soh*]
lieutenant, chūi [CHOO*'ee*]
(to) **lift,** mochiageru [*moh-chee'ah-gheh-roo*]
   (mochiagemasu)
light (electric), denki [*dehn-kee*]
light (not heavy), karui [*kah-rwee*]
(to) **like,** suki desu [*soo-kee dehss*]
   Do you like it? Suki desu ka?
   I don't like it. Suki de wa arimasen.
line, sen [*sehn*]

linen, rinneru [*reen-neh-roo*]

lingerie, rinneru seihin [*reen-neh-roo seh'ee-heen*]

lion, shishi [*shee-shee*]

lip, kuchibiru [*koo-chee-bee-roo*]

lipstick, kuchibeni [*koo-chee-beh-nee*]

liquor, sake [*sah-keh*]

list, hyō [*h'*YOH]

little, chiisai [*chee'ee-sah'ee*]

  a little, shukoshi [*shoo-koh-shee*]

(to) **live,** sumu [*soo-moo*] (sumimasu)

  Where do you live? Doko ni sunde imasu ka? [*Doh-koh nee soon-deh ee-mahss kah?*]

  long live, nagaiki [*nah-gah'ee-kee*]

liver, kanzō [*kahn-*ZOH]

lobby, hiroma [*hee-roh-mah*]

lobster, ise ebi [*ee-seh eh-bee*]

location, basho [*bah-shoh*]

locomotive, kikansha [*kee-kahn-shah*]

long, nagai [*nah-gah'ee*]

longer, yori nagai [*yoh-ree nah-gah'ee*]

(to) **look,** miru [*mee-roo*] (mimasu)

  Look! Goran nasai! [*Goh-rahn nah-sah'ee!*]

  Look out! Chūi! [CHOO'*ee!*]

loose, yurui [*yoo-roo'ee*]

(to) **lose,** nakusu [*nah-kooss*] (nakushimasu)

lost, nakushimashita [*nahk-shee-mahsh-tah*]

loud, ōgoe [OH-*goh-eh*]

loudspeaker, kakuseiki [*kah-koo-seh'ee-kee*]

love, aijō [*ah'ee-*JOH]

(to) **love,** aisu [*ah'ee-soo*] (aishimasu)

low, hikui [*hee-koo'ee*]

(to) **lubricate,** abura wo sasu [*ah-boo-rah woh sah-soo*] (abura wo sashimasu)

luck, ún [*oon*]
  Good luck! Gokoun wo inorimasu! [*Goh-koh-oon woh een-oh-ree-mahss!*]
lunch, chūshoku [CHOO-*shoh-koo*]
lung, hai [*hah'ee*]
luxurious, zeitaku na [*zeh'ee-tah-koo nah*]

machine, kikai [*kee-kah'ee*]
madam, okusan [*oh-koo-sahn*]
made, tsukutta [*tsoo-koot-tah*]
magazine, zasshi [*zahs-shee*]
maid, jochū [*joh*-CHOO]
mail, yūbin [YOO-*bin*]
main, shuyō na [*shoo*-YOH *nah*]
majority, daitasū [*dah'ee-tah*-SOO]
Malaya, Marai [*Mah-rah'ee*]
(to) make, tsukuru [*tsoo-koo-roo*] (tsukurimasu)
man, otoko [*oh-toh-koh*]
manager, shihainin [*shee-hah'ee-neen*]
manicure, manikyua [*mah-nee-k'yoo-ah*]
manner, sahō [*sah*-HOH]
(to) manufacture, seizō suru [*seh'ee*-ZOH *soo-roo*] (seizō shimasu)
many, takusan no [*tah-koo-sahn noh*]
map, chizu [*chee-zoo*]
marble, dairiseki [*dah'ee-ree-seh-kee*]
mark, shirushi [*shee-roo-shee*]
market, ichiba [*ee-chee-bah*]
married, kekkon shita [*kehk-kohn shee'tah*]
(to) marry, to kekkon suru [*toh kehk-kohn soo-roo*] (to kekkon shimasu)
marvelous, shubarashii [*shoo-bah-rah-shee'ee*]
master, shujin [*shoo-jeen*]
masterpieces, kessaku [*kehs-sah-koo*]
match, matchi [*maht-chee*]

material, zairyō [*zah'ee-r'YOH*]
  It does not matter, Kamaimasen [*kah-mah'ee-mah-sehn*]
  What's the matter? Doshita no desu ka? [*Doh-shee-tah noh dehss kah?*]
May, Gogatsu [*Goh-gaht-soo*]
mayonnaise, mayonezu [*mah-yoh-neh-zoo*]
me, watakushi wo [*wah-tahk-shee woh*]
  (to) me, watakushi ni [*wah-tahk-shee nee*]
  (with) me, watakushi to [*wah-tahk-shee toh*]
  (from) me, watakushi kara [*wah-tahk-shee kah-rah*]
meal, shokuji [*shoh-koo-jee*]
(to) mean, imi [*ee-mee*]
  What does it mean? Dō yū imi desu ka? [*DOH YOO ee-mee dehss kah?*]
(to) measure, hakaru [*hah-kah-roo*] (hakarimasu)
meat, niku [*nee-koo*]
mechanic, shurinin [*shoo-ree-nin*]
medal, metaru [*meh-tah-roo*]
medicine, kusuri [*koo-soo-ree*]
(to) meet, au [*ah-oo*]
  I am pleased to meet you! Hajimemashite! [*hah-jee-meh-mah-shee-teh!*]
melon, meron [*meh-rohn*]
member, kaiin [*kah'ee-een*]
memory, kioku [*kee'oh-koo*]
men's room, benjo [*behn-joh*]
menu, kondate hyō [*kohn-dah-teh h'YOH*]
merchant, zakka [*zahk-kah*]
message, kotozute [*koh-toh-zoo-teh*]
messenger, tsukai [*tsoo-kah'ee*]
metal, kinzoku [*kin-zoh-koo*]
middle, chūkan [*CHOO-kahn*]

mile—Miles are not used in Japan. **Kilometers,** kiro-
metoru; approximately 5/8 of a mile, are the
unit measure for distance.

milk, gyūnyū [g'YOO-n'YOO]

million, hyaku man [h'yah-koo mahn]

mind, kokoro [koh-koh-roh]

mine, watakushi no [wah-tahk-shee noh]

mineral, kobutsu [koh-boot-soo]

minute, fun [foon]

mirror, kagami [kah-gah-mee]

mistake, machigai [mah-chee-gah'ee]

(to) **mix,** mazeru [mah-zeh-roo] (mazemasu)

mixed, kongō shita [kohn-GOH sh'tah]

model, moderu [moh-deh-roo]

modern, modan [moh-dahn]

moment, chotto [choht-toh]

Monday, Getsyōbi [Gets-YOH-bee]

money, okane [oh-kah-neh]

monk, sōryo [SOH-r'yoh]

monkey, saru [sah-roo]

month, gatsu [gaht-soo]

monument, kinen zo [kee-nehn zoh]

moon, tsuki [tsoo-kee]

more, motto [moht-toh]

morning, asa [ah-sah]

mosquito, ka [kah]

most, ichiban [ee-chee-bahn]

mother, (mine) haha [hah-hah]
  (yours) okā-san [oh-KAH-sahn]

motor, mōtā [MOH-TAH]

mountain, yama [yah-mah]

mouse, nezumi [neh-zoo-mee]

mouth, kuchi [koo-chee]

(to) **move** (something), ugokasu [oo-goh-kah-soo]
  (ugokashimasu)

movies, eiga [*eh'ee-gah*]
Mr., Mrs., Miss, -san (added to the *end* of the proper name) [*sahn*]
much, takusan [*tah-koo-sahn*]
mushrooms, kinoko [*kee-noh-koh*]
music, ongaku [*ohn-gah-koo*]
musician, ongakuka [*ohn-gah-koo-kah*]
must

To express **must,** add "nakereba narimasen" to the modified infinitive in the following fashion: If the verb ends in "ru," ("miru" **to see**), drop the "ru": "Mi nakereba narimasen." **I must see.** If the verb ends in "u," ("iku" **to go**), change "u" to "a": "Ika nakereba narimasen." **He must go.** If the verb is formed with "suru," ("benkyō-suru" **to study**), change the "suru" to "shi": "Benkyō shi nakereba narimasen." **I must study.**

mustache, hige [*hee-gheh*]
mustard, karashi [*kah-rah-shee*]
my, watakushi no [*wah-tahk-shee noh*]

nail (for hammer), kugi [*koo-jee*]
name, namae [*nah-mah-eh*]
napkin, napukin [*nahp-kin*]
narrow, semai [*seh-mah'ee*]
nation, kokumin [*koh-koo-meen*]
nationality, kokuminsei [*koh-koo-meen-seh'ee*]
native, kokuseki [*koh-koo-seh-kee*]
natural, shizen no mama no [*shee-zehn noh mah-mah noh*]

nature, shizen [*shee-zehn*]
naval, kaigun no [*kah-ee-goon noh*]
navy, kaigun [*kah'ee-goon*]
rear, chikaku [*chee-kah-koo*]
nearly, hotondo [*hoh-tohn-doh*]
necessary, hitsuyō [*heet-soo-*YOH]
  It's not necessary fu hitsuyō [*foo heet-soo-*YOH]
neck, kubi [*koo-bee*]
(to) need, iru [*ee-roo*] (irimasu)
needle, hari [*hah-ree*]
negro, kokujin [*koh-koo-jeen*]
neighbor, tonari no [*toh-nah-ree noh*]
neither one, dochiramo de nai [*doh-chee-rah-moh deh nah'ee*]
nephew, oi [*oh'ee*]
nerve, shinkei [*shin-keh'ee*]
nervous, shinkei no [*shin-keh'ee noh*]
Netherlands, Oranda [*Oh-ran-dah*]
Netherlands (person), Oranda-jin [*-jeen*]
Netherlands (language), Oranda-go [*-goh*]
never, mada [*mah-dah*]
never mind, kamaimasen [*kah-mah'ee-mah-sehn*]
nevertheless, soredemo [*soh-reh-deh-moh*]
new, atarashii [*ah-tah-rah-shee'ee*]
news, nyusu [*n'yoo-soo*]
newspaper, shimbun [*sheem-boon*]
next, tsugi no [*tsoo-ghee noh*]
nice, kekkō [*kehk-*KOH]
niece, mei [*meh'ee*]
night, yoru [*yoh-roo*]
nightgown, nemaki [*neh-mah-kee*]
nine, kū [KOO] or kyū [*k'*YOO]
nineteen, jūku [JOO-*koo*]
ninety, kyūjū [*k'*YOO-JOO]

no, iye [*ee-yeh*]
   It's no good. Sore wa yoku nai. [*Soh-reh wah
   yoh-koo nah'ee*]
nobody, daremo... [*dah-reh-moh*...] (following
   verb is in negative form)
noisy, sozoshii [*soh-zoh-shee'ee*]
none, nani mo... [*nah-nee moh*...] (followed by
   negative)
nonsense, tsumaranaikoto [*tsoo-mah-rah-nah'ee-
   koh-toh*]
north, kita [*kee-tah*]
North America, Kita Amerika [*Kee-tah Ah-meh-
   ree-kah*]
northeast, hokutō [*hoh-koo-*TOH]
northwest, hokusei [*hoh-koo-seh'ee*]
Norway, Nōruwei [NOH-*roo-weh'ee*]
nose, hana [*hah-nah*]
not, de nai [*deh nah'ee*]
notebook, chōmen [CHOH-*mehn*]
nothing, nani no nai [*nah-nee noh nah'ee*]
notice, tsūchi [*t'soo-chee*]
novelty, shinanbutsu [*shee-nahn-boot-soo*]
November, Juichigatsu [*Joo'ee-chee-gaht-soo*]
now, ima [*ee-mah*]
nuisance, yakkai [*yahk-kah'ee*]
number, sūji [*soo-jee*]
numerous, tasū no [*tah-soo noh*]
nurse, kangofu [*kahn-goh-foo*]
nursemaid, komori onna [*koh-moh-ree ohn-**nah**]
nut, ki no mi [*kee noh mee*]

(to) obtain, eru [*eh-roo*] (emasu)
obvious, akiraka [*ah-kee-rah-kah*]
occasionally, oriori [*oh-ree-oh-ree*]
occidental, seiyō no [*seh'ee-*YOH *noh*]

occupation, shōkugyō [SHOH-*koo*-g'YOH]
(to) **occupy,** senryō suru [*sehn-r'*YOH *soo-roo*]
  (senryō shimasu)
ocean, kaiyō [*kah'ee*-YOH]
o'clock, ji [*jee*]
October, Jūgatsu [JOO-*gaht-soo*]
odor, kaori [*kah-oh-ree*]
of, no [*noh*]
(to) **offer,** teikyō suru [*teh'ee-k'*YOH *soo-roo*]
office, jimusho [*jee-moo-shoh*]
officer (military), shikan [*shee-kahn*]
official, ooyake no [*oh'oh-yah-keh noh*]
often, shiba shiba [*shee-bah shee-bah*]
oil, abura [*ah-boo-rah*]
oil well, yuden [*yoo-dehn*]
old (for people), toshiyori [*toh-shee-yoh-ree*]
old (for things), furui [*foo-roo'ee*]
omelet, omuretsu [*oh-moo-reht-soo*]
on, no ue ni [*noh oo-eh nee*]
once, ichido [*ee-chee-doh*]
one, ichi [*ee-chee*] or hitotsu [*hee-toht-soo*]
onion, tamanegi [*tah-mah-neh-ghee*]
only, dake [*dah-keh*]
open, hiraita [*hee-rah'ee-tah*]
(to) **open,** akeru [*ah-keh-roo*] (akemasu)
opera, kageki [*kah-gheh-kee*]
operation (medical), shujutsu [*shoo-joot-soo*]
operator (telephone), kōkanshu [KOH-*kahn-shoo*]
opinion, iken [*ee-kehn*]
opportunity, kikai [*kee-kah'ee*]
opposite, sei hantai no [*seh'ee hahn-tah'ee noh*]
optician, megane ya [*meh-gah-neh ya*]
orange, mikan [*mee-kahn*]
orangeade, orenji sui [*oh-rehn-jee swee*]
orchard, kaju-en [*kah-joo-ehn*]

orchestra, kangengakudan [*kahn-ghehn-gah-koo-dahn*]
orient, tōyō [TOH-YOH]
oriental, tōyō no [TOH-YOH *noh*]
original, genbutsu no [*ghehn-boot-soo noh*]
orphan, koji [*koh-jee*]
other, hoka no [*hoh-kah noh*]
our, watakushitachi no [*wah-tahk-shee-tah-chee noh*]
outside, soto [*soh-toh*]
oven, kamado [*kah-mah-doh*]
overcoat, gaitō [*gah'ee-*TOH]
(to) owe, karite iru [*kah-ree-teh ee-roo*] (karite imasu)
owl, fukurō [*foo-koo-*ROH]
owner, mochinushi [*moh-chee-noo-shee*]
ox, ushi [*oo-shee*]
oyster, kaki [*kah-kee*]

Pacific Ocean, Taiheiyo [*Tah'ee-heh'ee-yoh*]
pack (of cards), kado hitokumi [*kah-doh hee-toh-koo-mee*]
(to) pack, tsutsumu [*tsoo-tsoo-moo*] (tsutsumi-masu)
package, kodzutsumi [*kohd-zoot-soo-mee*]
page, pēji [PEH'*jee*]
pagoda, tō [TOH]
pain, itami [*ee-tah-mee*]
(to) paint, penki wo nuru [*pehn-kee woh noo-roo*]
pair, hitokumi [*hee-toh-koo-mee*]
pajama, nemaki [*neh-mah-kee*]
palace, kyūden [k'YOO-*dehn*]
parasol, higasa [*hee-gah-sah*]
pardon, yurushi [*yoo-roo-shee*]
parents, ryōshin [r'YOH-*shin*]

park, kōen [KOH-*ehn*]
(to) **park,** chūsha suru [CHOO-*shah soo-roo*]
  (chūsha shimasu)
parrot, oumu [*oh-oo-moo*]
parsley, paseri [*pah-seh-ree*]
part, bubun [*boo-boon*]
part (of a machine), buhin [*boo-heen*]
particular, tokubetsu no [*toh-koo-beht-soo noh*]
partner, nakama [*nah-kah-mah*]
party, kai [*kah'ee*]
(to) **pass,** tsūka suru [TSOO-*kah soo-roo*] (tsūka
  shimasu)
passage, tsūkō [TSOO-KOH]
passenger, jōkyaku [JOH-*k'yah-koo*]
passport, ryoken [*r'yoh-kehn*]
past, kako no [*kah-koh noh*]
patent, tokkyo [*tohk-k'yoh*]
(to) **pay,** shiharau [*shee-hah-rah-oo*] (shiharai-
  masu)
  (to) **pay cash,** genkin wo shiharau [*ghehn-kin
  woh shee-hah-rah-oo*]
payment, shiharai [*shee-hah-rah'ee*]
pea, endō mame [*ehn*-DOH *mah-meh*]
peace, heiwa [*heh'ee-wah*]
peach, momo [*moh-moh*]
peanut, nankin mame [*nahn-kin mah-meh*]
pear, nasi [*nah-see*]
pearl, shinju [*shin-joo*]
peculiar, dokutoku no [*doh-koo-toh-koo noh*]
penalty, shobatsu [*shoh-baht-soo*]
pencil, enputsu [*ehn-poot-soo*]
people, hitobito [*hee-toh-bee-toh*]
pepper, koshō [*koh*-SHOH]
  green pepper, pīman [PEE-*mahn*]
perfect, kanzen na [*kahn-zehn nah*]

perfume, kōsui [KOH-*swee*]
perhaps, tabun [*tah-boon*]
period, jiki [*jee-kee*]
permanent, eikyū no [*eh-eek'*YOO *noh*]
(to) **permit,** kyoka suru [*k'yoh-kah soo-roo*]
  (kyoka shimasu)
peroxide, kasankabutsu [*kah-sahn-kah-boot-soo*]
person, hito [*hee-toh*]
personal, kojin no [*koh-jeen noh*]
perspiration, ase [*ah-seh*]
Philippines, Fuirippin [*Foo'ee-reep-peen*]
Filipino (person), Fuirippin-jin
philosopher, tetsugakusha [*teht-soo-gahk-shah*]
phonograph, chikuonki [*chee-koo-ohn-kee*]
(to) **take a photo,** shashin wo toru [*shah-shin woh toh-roo*] (shashin wo torimasu)
pie, pai [*pah'ee*]
piece, ikko [*eek-koh*]
pier, sanbashi [*sahn-bah-shee*]
pig, buta [*boo-tah*]
pigeon, hato [*hah-toh*]
pile, kui [*kwee*]
pill, ganyaku [*gahn-yah-koo*]
pillow, makura [*mah-koo-rah*]
pilot, sōjūshi [SOH-JOO-*shee*]
pin, pin [*peen*]
pink, momo iro [*moh-moh ee-roh*]
pipe, tsutsu [*t'soo-t'soo*]
pipe (for smoking), paipu [*pah'ee-poo*]
place, basho [*bah-shoh*]
plain, tanjun na [*tahn-joon nah*]
plan, keika [*keh'ee-kah*]
plastic, purasuchiku [*prahss-cheek-koo*]
plate, sara [*sah-rah*]
please, dōzo [DOH-*zoh*]
pleasure, tanoshimi [*tahn-oh-shee-mee*]

plenty, takusan [*tahk-sahn*]

plum, sumono [*soo-moh-noh*]

pneumonia, haien [*hah'ee-ehn*]

pocket, poketto [*poh-keht-toh*]

pocket-book, techō [*teh-*CHOH]

poem, shi [*shee*]

poet, shijin [*shee-jeen*]

point, ten [*tehn*]

poison, doku [*doh-koo*]

police, keisatsu [*keh'ee-sat-soo*]

political, seiji no [*seh'ee-jee noh*]

pond, ike [*ee-keh*]

pool, pūru [POO-*roo*]

poor, binbō [*been-*BOH]

pork, buta niku [*boo-tah nee-koo*]

port, minato [*mee-nah-toh*]

portrait, shōzō [SHOH-ZOH]

Portugal, Porutogaru [*Pohr-toh-gah-roo*]

Portuguese (language), Porutugaru-go

Portuguese (person), Porutugaru-jin

position, chii [*chee'ee*]

    Is it possible? Kanō desu ka? [*Kah-*NOH *dehss kah?*]

post office, yūbin kyoku [YOO-*been k'yoh-koo*]

postage, yūbin ryōkin [YOO-*been r'*YOH-*keen*]

postage stamp, yūbin kitte [YOO-*been kit-teh*]

post card, hagaki [*hah-gah-kee*]

potato, jagaimo [*jah-gah'ee-moh*]

powder, kona [*koh-nah*]

powerful, yūryoku na [YOO-*r'yoh-koo nah*]

practice, renshū [*rehn-*SHOO]

precious, kōka na [KOH-*kah nah*]

(to) prefer, no ho wo konomu [*noh hoh woh koh-noh-moo*] (no ho wo konomimasu)

pregnant, ninshin shiteiru [*neen-shin shee-teh'ee-roo*]

premier, saisho no *[sah'ee-shoh noh]*

preparation, shitaku *[shee-tah-koo]*

prescription, shohō *[shoh-HOH]*

present (gift), okurimono *[oh-koo-ree-moh-noh]*
  (time), genzai no *[ghehn-zah'ee noh]*

(to) **press** (cloth), puresu wo suru *[prehss woh soo-roo]*

pretty, kawaii *[kah-wah'ee]*

(to) **prevent,** yobō suru *[yoh-BOH soo-roo]*

previous, mae no *[mah-eh noh]*

price, nedan *[neh-dahn]*

priest, shinpu *[shin-poo]*

prince, kōtaishi *[KOH-tah'ee-shee]*

princess, kōtaishihi *[KOH-tah'ee-shee-hee]*

prints (Japanese), hanga *[hahn-gah]*

prison, keimusho *[keh'ee-moo-shoh]*

prisoner, shūjin *[SHOO-jeen]*

private, shiyō no *[shee-YOH noh]*

prize, shōhin *[SHOH-heen]*

problem, mondai *[mohn-dah'ee]*

(to) **produce,** seisan suru *[seh'ee-sahn soo-roo]*
  (seisan shimasu)

production, seisan *[seh'ee-sahn]*

profession, shokugyō *[shoh-koo-g'YOH]*

professor, kyōju *[k'YOH-joo]*

profit, rieki *[ree-eh-kee]*

program, puroguramu *[proh-grah-moo]*

(to) **progress,** zenshin suru *[zehn-shin soo-roo]*
  (zenshin shimasu)

promise, yakusoku *[yah-koo-soh-koo]* (yakusokimasu)

prompt, binsoku na *[been-soh-koo nah]*

pronunciation, hatsuon *[haht-soo-ohn]*

proof, shōko *[SHOH-koh]*

propaganda, senden *[sehn-dehn]*

property, zaisan *[zah'ee-sahn]*

proposal, teian [*teh'ee-ahn*]

proprietor, shoyūshu [*shoh*-YOO-*shoo*]

prosperity, hanjō [*hahn*-JOH]

(to) **protect,** mamoru [*mah-moh-roo*] (mamori-masu)

protection, hogo [*hoh-goh*]

Protestant, shinkyō no [*shin-k'*YOH *noh*]

province, chihō [*chee*-HOH]

provincial, chihō no [*chee*-HOH *noh*]

(to) **prune,** karitoru [*kah-ree-toh-roo*] (karitori-masu)

psychiatrist, seishinbyōgakusha [*seh'ee-shin-b'*YOH-*gah-koo-shah*]

public, ōyake no [OH-*yah-keh noh*]

(to) **publish,** shuppan suru [*shoop-pahn soo-roo*] (shuppan shimasu)

publishing house, shuppan sha [*shoop-pahn shah*]

(to) **pull,** hiku [*hee-koo*] (hikimasu)

pump, ponpu [*pohn-poo*]

(to) **punish,** bassuru [*bahs-soo-roo*] (basshimasu)

pupil, seito [*seh'ee-toh*]

(to) **purchase,** kau [*kah-oo*] (kaimasu)

pure, junsui [*joon-swee*]

purple, murasaki [*moo-rah-sah-kee*]

(to) **push,** oshu [*oh-shoo*] (oshimasu)

(to) **put,** oku [*oh-koo*] (okimasu)

quality, hinsitsu [*heen-sit-soo*]

quantity, bunryō [*boon-r'*YOH]

quarrel, kenka [*kehn-kah*]

quarter, yonbun no ichi [*yohn-boon noh ee-chee*]

queen, jōō [JOH-OH]

question, shitsumon [*shit-soo-mohn*]

To ask a question in Japanese,

remember to use "ka" after the
polite form of the verb. Example:
"Kore desu ka?" Is this it?

quick, hayai [*hah-yah'ee*]
quickly, hayaku [*hah-yah-koo*]
quiet, shizuka [*shee-zoo-kah*]
  Be quiet! shizuka ni! [*shee-zoo-kah nee!*]
(to) **quit,** chushi suru [*choo-shee soo-roo*] (chushi
  shimasu)
quite, mattaku [*maht-tah-koo*]
quilt, kakebuton [*kah-keh-boo-tohn*]

rabbit, usagi [*oo-sah-ghee*]
race, kyōsō [*k'YOH-SOH*]
radiator, reikyakuki [*reh'ee-k'yah-koo-kee*]
radio, rajio [*rah-jee-oh*]
railroad, tetsudō [*teht-soo-DOH*]
rain, ame [*ah-meh*]
(to) **raise,** ageru [*ah-geh-roo*] (agemasu)
raisin, hoshibudō [*hoh-shee-boo-DOH*]
rank, kaikyū [*kah'ee-k'YOO*]
rapid, sumiyaka na [*soo-mee-yah-kah nah*]
rapidly, sumiyaka ni [*soo-mee-yah-kah nee*]
rat (*or*) **mouse,** nezumi [*neh-zoo-mee*]
rate, buai [*boo-ah'ee*]
rather, mushiro [*moo-shee-roh*]
raw material, genryō [*ghehn-r'YOH*]
razor, kamisori [*kah-mee-soh-ree*]
razor blade, kamisori no ha [*kah-mee-soh-ree noh
  hah*]
(to) **reach,** todoku [*toh-doh-koo*] (todokimasu)
(to) **read,** yomu [*yoh-moo*] (yomimasu)
ready, yōi no dekita [*YOH'ee noh deh-kee-tah*]
  Is it ready? Sumimashita ka? [*soo-mee-mah-
  shee-tah kah?*]

real, shinjitsu [*shin-jeet-soo*]

really, jissai ni [*jees-sah'ee nee*]

rear, haigo [*hah'ee-goh*]

reason, riyū [*ree-*YOO]

reasonable, dato [*dah-toh*]

receipt, ryōshūsho [*r'*YOH-SHOO-*shoh*]

(to) **receive,** uketoru [*oo-keh-toh-roo*] (uketori-masu)

recent, saikin no [*sah'ee-kin noh*]

recipe, shoho [*shoh-hoh*]

(to) **recognize,** mitomeru [*mee-toh-meh-roo*] (mitomemasu)

(to) **recommend,** suisen suru [*swee-sehn soo-roo*] (suisen shimasu)

record, kiroku [*kee-roh-koo*]

record player, recōdo pureyā [*reh-*KOH-*doh preh-*YAH]

(to) **recover,** kaifuku suru [*kah'ee-foo-koo soo-roo*] (kaifuku shimasu)

red, aka [*ah-kah*]

(to) **reduce,** herasu [*hehrahss*] (herashimasu)

reduction, waribiki [*wah-ree-bee-kee*]

reef, anshō [*ahn-*SHOH]

refrigerator, reizōko [*reh-*ZOH-*koh*]

(to) **regret,** zannen ni omou [*zahn-nehn nee oh-moh'oo*] (zannen ni omoimasu)

regular, teikiteki na [*teh'ee-kee-teh-kee nah*]

relative, shinseki [*shin-seh-kee*]

religion, shūkyō [SHOO-*k'*YOH]

remark, hihyō [*hee-h'*YOH]

remedy, ryoho [*r'yoh-hoh*]

(to) **remember,** omoidasu [*oh-moh'ee-dahss*] (omoidashimasu)

(to) **remove,** iten suru [*ee-tehn soo-roo*] (iten shimasu)

rent, yachin [*yah-chin*]

(to) **rent,** kariru [*kah-ree-roo*] (karimasu)

(to) **repair,** shūri suru [SHOO-*ree soo-roo*] (shūri shimasu)

(to) **repeat,** kurikaesu [*koo-ree-kah-ehss*] (kuri-kaeshimasu)

(to) **represent,** daihyō suru [*dah'ee-h'*YOH *soo-roo*] (daihyō shimasu)

representative, daihyōsha [*dah'ee-h'*YOH-*shah*]

reproduction, fukusha [*foo-koo-shah*]

republic, kyōwakoku [*k'*YOH-*wah-koh-koo*]

(to) **request,** irai suru [*ee-rah'ee soo-roo*] [irai shimasu]

(to) **rescue,** kyūjo suru [*k'*YOO-*joh soo-roo*] (kyūjo shimasu)

(to) **reserve,** yoyaku suru [*yoh-yah-koo soo-roo*] (yoyaku shimasu)

reserved, yoyaku no [*yoh-yah-koo noh*]

reservoir, chosuichi [*choh-swee-chee*]

residence, kyoju [*k'yoh-joo*]

resident, ijū suru [*ee-*JOO *soo-roo*]

respect, sonkei [*sohn-keh'ee*]

respectable, sonkei subeki [*sohn-keh'ee soo-beh-kee*]

responsible, sekinin [*seh-kee-neen*]

rest, kyūsoku [*k'*YOO-*soh-koo*]

(to) **rest,** yasumu [*yah-soo-moo*] (yasumimasu)

restaurant, riyoriya [*ree-yoh-ree-yah*]

restless, ochitsukanai [*oh-cheet-soo-kah-nah'ee*]

result, kekka [*kehk-kah*]

retired, taishoku shita [*tah'ee-shoh-koo shee-tah*]

(to) **return** (to go back), kaeru [*kah-eh-roo*] (kaerimasu)

(to) **return** (to give back), kaesu [*kah-eh-soo*] (kaeshimasu)

review, fukushū [*foo-koo-*SHOO]

revolution, kakumei [*kah-koo-meh'ee*]
reward, hōshū [HOH-SHOO]
rib, abara bone [*ah-bah-rah boh-neh*]
rice, kome [*koh-meh*]
rice crackers, senbei [*sehn-beh'ee*]
rich, kanemochi [*kah-neh-moh-chee*]
(to) **ride,** noru [*noh-roo*] (norimasu)
rifle, shōju [SHOH-*joo*]
right (correct), tadashii [*tah-dah-shee'ee*]
right (direction), migi [*mee-ghee*]
  to the right! migi e! [*mee-ghee eh!*]
ring, yubiwa [*yoo-bee-wah*]
rising sun, asahi [*ah-sah'ee*]
river, kawa [*kah-wah*]
road, michi [*mee-chee*]
(to) **roast,** aburu [*ah-boo-roo*] (aburimasu)
(to) **rob,** ubau [*oo-bah'oo*] (ubaimasu)
robber, gōtō [GOH-TOH]
rock, iwa [*ee-wah*]
romantic, romanchik-ku [*roh-mahn-cheek-koo*]
roof, yane [*yah-neh*]
room, heya [*heh-yah*]
rope, nawa [*nah-wah*]
rose, bara [*bah-rah*]
rouge, beni [*beh-nee*]
rough, arai [*ah-rah'ee*]
round, marui [*mah-roo'ee*]
royal, kokuō no [*koh-koo-*OH *noh*]
ruby, rubī [*roo-*BEE]
rug, jūtan [JOO-*tahn*]
ruin, metsubō [*met-soo-*BOH]
rum, ramushu [*rah-moo-shoo*]
(to) **run,** hashiru [*hah-shee-roo*] (hashirimasu)
Russia Roshiya [*Roh-shee-yah*]
Russian (language), Roshiya-go
Russian (person), Roshiya-jin

sad, kanashii [*kah-nah-shee'ee*]
saddle, kura [*koo-rah*]
safe, anzen [*ahn-zehn*]
said, jōjutsu no [JOH-*joo-t'soo noh*]
sailor, suihei [*swee-heh'ee*]
saint, seijin [*seh'ee-jeen*]
salad, sarada [*sah-rah-dah*]
salesman, tenin [*teh-neen*]
saleslady, jo tenin [*joh teh-neen*]
salmon, sāke [SAH-*keh*]
salt, shio [*shee-oh*]
same, onaji [*oh-nah-jee*]
sand, suna [*soo-nah*]
sandals (flat), zori [*zoh-ree*]
sandals (wooden), geta [*geh-tah*]
sandwich, sandoichi [*sahn-doh'ee-chee*]
sapphire, safaiya [*sah-fah'ee-yah*]
sash, obi [*oh-bee*]
satisfactory, manzoku na [*mahn-zoh-koo nah*]
satisfied, manzoku shita [*mahn-zoh-koo shee-tah*]
Saturday, Doyōbi [*Doh*-YOH-*bee*]
sauce, sōsu [SOH-*soo*]
sausage, sōsēji [SOH-SEH-*jee*]
(to) save (rescue), tasukeru [*tahss-keh-roo*] (tasu-kemasu)
(to) say, yū [YOO] (iimasu)
scar, kizuato [*kee-zoo-ah-toh*]
scarf, sukāfu [*soo-*KAH-*foo*]
scarlet, fukabeni iro [*foo-kah-beh-nee ee-roh*]
schedule, yoteihyō [*yoh-teh'ee-h'*YOH]
school, gakkō [*gah-*KOH]
schoolteacher, gakko no kyoshi [*gah-koh noh k'yoh-shee*]
science, kagaku [*kah-gah-koo*]
scientific, kagakuteki [*kah-gah-koo-teh-kee*]
scientist, kagakusha [*kah-gah-koo-shah*]

scissors, hasami [*hah-sah-mee*]

(to) scratch, kaku [*kah-koo*] (kakimasu)

scream, himei [*hee-meh'ee*]

screen, byōbu [*b'*YOH-*boo*]

scroll, kakegiku [*kah-keh-ghee-koo*]

screw, neji [*neh-jee*]

sea, umi [*oo-mee*]

seam, nuime [*noo'ee-meh*]

seaport, hatoba [*hah-toh-bah*]

(to) search, sagasu [*sah-gahss*] (sagashimasu)

season, kisetsu [*kee-set-soo*]

seat, seki [*seh-kee*]

second (time), byō [*b'*YOH]

second (order), nibunne no [*nee-boon-neh noh*]

secret, himitsu [*hee-meet-soo*]

secretary, hisho [*hee-shoh*]

(to) see, miru [*mee-roo*] (mimasu)

(to) seem, omowareru [*oh-moh-wah-reh-roo*] (omowaremasu)

(to) select, erabu [*eh-rah-boo*] (erabimasu)

(to) sell, uru [*oo-roo*] (urimasu)

(to) send, okuru [*oh-koo-roo*] (okurimasu)

sensible, kenmei [*kehn-meh'ee*]

sensitive, kanjiyasui [*kahn-jee-yah-swee*]

sentence, bun [*boon*]

sentimental, senchimentaru [*sehn-chee-mehn-tah-roo*]

September, Kugatsu [*Koo-gaht-soo*]

series, renzoku [*rehn-zoh-koo*]

sergeant, gunsō [*goon-*SOH]

serious (thoughtful), majime na [*mah-jee-meh nah*]

service, sābisu [SAH-*beess*]

(to) set, haichi suru [*hah'ee-chee soo-roo*] (haichi shimasu)

seven, shichi [*shee-chee*] or nanatsu [*nah-nah-tsoo*]

seventeen, jūshichi [JOO-*shee-chee*]

seventh, nana banme no [*nah-nah bahn-meh noh*]

seventy, nanju [*nah-nah-joo*] or shichijū [*shee-chee-*JOO]

several, ikutsuka no [*ee-koot-soo-kah noh*]

severe, genkaku na [*gehn-kah-koo nah*]

(to) sew, nuu [*noo-oo*] (nuimasu)

shade, kage [*kah-gheh*]

shall, see "will"

shape, katachi [*kah-tah-chee*]

shark, same [*sah-meh*]

sharp, surudoi [*soo-roo-doh'ee*]

(to) shave, hige wo soru [*hee-gheh woh soh-roo*] (hige wo sorimasu)

she, kanojo [*kah-noh-joh*]

sheep, hitsuji [*hit-soo-jee*]

sheet, shikifu [*shee-kee-foo*]

shell, kara [*kah-rah*]

shell fish, kai [*kah'ee*]

sherry, sherī [*sheh-*REE]

ship, fune [*foo-neh*]

  (to) send by ship, fune de okuru [*foo-neh deh oh-koo-roo*] (fune de okurimasu)

shirt, shatsu [*shaht-soo*]

shock, kutsushita [*koot-soo-shee-tah*]

shoe, kutsu [*koot-soo*]

shoemaker, kutsu-ya [*koot-soo-yah*]

(to) shoot, utsu [*oot-soo*] (uchimasu)

shop, mise [*mee-seh*]

short, mijikai [*mee-jee-kah'ee*]

shoulder, kata [*kah-tah*]

(to) show, miseru [*mee-seh-roo*] (misemasu)

  Show me! Misete kudasai! [*Mee-seh-teh koo-dah-sah'ee!*]

show (theater), shibai [*shee-bah'ee*]
shower, yūdachi [YOO-*dah-chee*]
shrimp, chisai ebi [*chee-sah'ee eh-bee*]
shrine, jinja [*jeen-jah*]
(to) **shut,** shimaru [*shee-mah-roo*] (shimemasu)
shy, uchiki na [*oo-chee-kee nah*]
sick, byōki no [*b'*YOH-*kee noh*]
sickness, byōki [*b'*YOH-*kee*]
side, gawa [*gah-wah*]
sidewalk, hodō [*hoh-*DOH]
sight, shiryoku [*shee-r'yoh-koo*]
  sight-seeing, kankō [*kan-*KOH]
silence, chinmoku [*chin-moh-koo*]
silk, kinu [*kee-noo*]
silly, oroka na [*oh-roh-kah nah*]
silver, gin [*gheen*]
similar, dōyō no [DOH-YOH *noh*]
simple, kantan na [*kahn-tahn nah*]
since, sono go [*soh-noh goh*]
(to) **sing,** utau [*oo-tah-oo*] (utaimàsu)
single, tanitsu na [*tah-neet-soo nah*]
sister, shimai [*shee-mah'ee*]
  my elder sister, ane [*ah-neh*]
  my younger sister, imōto [*ee-*MOHT-*oh*]
  your elder sister, onē san [*oh-*NEH *sahn*]
  your younger sister, imōto-san [*ee-*MOHT-*oh sahn*]
shaving cream, hige sori kurīmu [*hee-gheh soh-ree koo-*REE-*moo*]
(to) **sit,** suwaru (Japanese fashion) [*soo-wah-roo*] (suwarimasu)
(to) **sit,** koshikakeru (Western fashion) [*koh-shee-kah-keh-roo*] (koshikakemasu)
sitting, zaseki [*zah-seh-kee*]
situation, jōkyō [JOH-*k'yoh*]
six, roku [*roh-koo*] or muttsu [*moot-tsoo*]

sixteen, jūroku [JOO-*roh-koo*]
sixth, rokuban me [*roh-koo-bahn meh*]
sixty, roku ju [*roh-koo joo*]
size, sunpō [*soon*-POH]
skin, hifu [*hee-foo*]
skirt, sukāto [*soo*-KAH-*toh*]
sky, sora [*soh-rah*]
skyscraper, matenrō [*mah-tehn*-ROH]
(to) sleep, nemuru [*neh-moo-roo*] (nemurimasu)
sleeve, sode [*soh-deh*]
slight, shukoshi no [*shoo-koh-shee noh*]
slippery, tsuru tsuru suberu [*tsoo-roo tsoo-roo soo-beh-roo*]
slow, osoi [*oh-soh'ee*]
slowly, yukkuri [*yook-koo-ree*]
small, chiisai [*chee'ee-sah'ee*]
smell, nioi [*nee-oh'ee*]
(to) smell, kagu [*kah-goo*] (kagimasu)
Smile please! Waratte kudasai! [*Wah-raht-teh koo-dah-sah'ee!*]
smoke, kemuri [*keh-moo-ree*]
(to) smoke, tabako wo suu [*tah-bah-koh woh soo'oo*] (tabako wo suimasu)
smooth, taira na [*tah'ee-rah nah*]
snake, hebi [*heh-bee*]
snow, yuki [*yoo-kee*]
snowstorm, fubuki [*foo-boo-kee*]
so, sonoyōni [*soh-noh*-YOH-*nee*]
so long, sayōnara [*sah*-YOH-*nah-rah*]
soap, sekken [*sehk-kehn*]
socialist, shakai shugisha [*shah-kah'ee shoo-ghee-shah*]
society, kyōkai [*k'*YOH-*kah'ee*]
sock, kutsushita [*koot-soo-shee-tah*]
soda, sōdā [SOH-DAH]
soft, yawaraka na [*yah-wah-rah-kah nah*]

sold, ureta [*oo-reh-tah*]
soldier, gunjin [*goon-jeen*]
solid, katai [*kah-tah'ee*]
some, ikuraka no [*ee-koo-rah-kah noh*]
somebody, dare ka [*dah-reh kah*]
something, nani ka [*nah-nee kah*]
sometime, itsu ka [*it-soo kah*]
sometimes, toki doki [*toh-kee doh-kee*]
somewhat, ikura ka [*ee-koo-rah kah*]
somewhere, doko ka [*doh-koh kah*]
(my) **son,** musuko [*moos-koh*]
(your) **son,** musuko-san [*moos-koh sahn*]
song, uta [*oo-tah*]
soon, sugu [*soo-goo*]
sore, haremono [*hah-reh-moh-noh*]
sore throat, inkōen [*in-*KOH*-ehn*]
sorry, kawaishōde [*kah-wah-ee-*SHOH *deh*]
  I am sorry! Gomen nasai! [*Goh-mehn nah-sah'ee!*]
sort, shurui [*shoo-roo'ee*]
sound, oto [*oh-toh*]
South America, Minami Amerika [*Mee-nah-mee Ah-meh-ree-kah*]
souvenir, miyage [*mee-yah-gheh*]
space, kūkan [KOO-*kahn*]
Spain, Supein [*Soo-pane*]
Spanish (person), Supein-jin
Spanish (language), Supein-go
(to) **speak,** hanasu [*hah-nah-soo*] (hanashimasu)
special, tokubetsu no [*toh-koo-beht-soo noh*]
speed, sokudo [*soh-koo-doh*]
spider, kumo [*koo-moh*]
spine, sebone [*seh-boh-neh*]
splendid, rippa na [*reep-pah nah*]
spoon, saji [*sah-jee*]

sport, supōtsu [SPOHT-*soo*]

spot, ten [*tehn*]

spring (season), haru [*hah-roo*]

spring (metal coil), bane [*bah-neh*]

square, seihōkei [*seh'ee*-HOH-*keh'ee*]

stairs, kaidan [*kah'ee-dahn*]

stamp, kitte [*kit-teh*]

(to) **stand,** tatsu [*taht-soo*] (tachimasu)

standing, tatte iru [*taht-teh ee-roo*]

star, hoshi [*hoh-shee*]

starch, nori [*noh-ree*]

(to) **start,** hajimeru [*hah-jee-meh-roo*] (hajime-masu)

stateroom, tokubetsu shitsu [*toh-koo-beht-soo sheet-soo*]

station, eki [*eh-kee*]

statue, zō [ZOH]

(to) **stay,** todomaru [*toh-doh-mah-roo*] (todomari-masu)

steak, sutēki [*soo*-TEH-*kee*]

(to) **steal,** nusumu [*noo-soo-moo*] (nusumimasu)

steam, jōki [JOH-*kee*]

stenographer, sokkisha [*sohk-kee-shah*]

step, ayumi [*ah-yoo-mee*]

(to) **sterilize,** shōdoku suru [SHOH-*doh-koo soo-roo*] (shōdoku shimasu)

steward, kyūji [*k'YOO-jee*]

stewardess, suchuwadesu [*soo-choo-wah-dehss*]

stick, bō [BOH]

stiff, kitsui [*kit-swee*]

(to) **stimulate,** shigeki suru [*shee-gheh-kee soo-roo*] (shigeki shimasu)

(to) **sting,** sasu [*sah-soo*] (sashimasu)

stomach, i [*ee*]

stone, ishi [*ee-shee*]

(to) **stop,** tomaru [*toh-mah-roo*] (tomarimasu)

Stop! Tomarinasai! [*Toh-mah-ree-nah-sah'ee!*]
Stop thief! Dorobō mate! [*Doh-roh-*BOH *mah-teh!*]
store, shōten [SHOH-*tehn*]
storm, arashi [*ah-rah-shee*]
story, hanashi [*hah-nah-shee*]
straight, massugu [*mahs-soo-goo*]
  straight ahead, massugu ni [*mahs-soo-goo nee*]
strange, fushigi na [*foo-shee-ghee nah*]
straw, wara [*wah-rah*]
stream, nagare [*nah-gah-reh*]
street, tori [TOH-*ree*]
streetcar, shinai densha [*shee-nah'ee dehn-shah*]
strength, chikara [*chee-kah-rah*]
string, himo [*hee-moh*]
strong, tsuyoi [*tsoo-yoh'ee*]
student, gakusei [*gahk-seh'ee*]
(to) study, benkyō suru [*behn-k'*YOH *soo-roo*]
  (benkyō shimasu)
style, sutairu [*stah'ee-roo*]
suburb, kōgai [KOH-*gah'ee*]
subway, chikatetsu [*chee-kah-teht-soo*]
success, seikō [*seh'ee-*KOH]
such, son na [*sohn nah*]
suddenly, kyū ni [*k'*YOO *nee*]
sufficient, jūbun na [JOO-*boon nah*]
sugar, satō [*sah-*TOH]
suicide, jisatsu [*jee-saht-soo*]
suit, sūtsu [SOO-*t'soo*]
summer, natsu [*naht-soo*]
sun, taiyō [*tah'ee-*YOH]
Sunday, Nichiyōbi [*Nee-chee-*YOH-*bee*]
sure, tashika [*tah-shee-kah*]
surgeon, geka [*gheh-kah*]
Sweden, Suēden [*Soo-*EH-*den*]
Swedish (language), Suēden-go

Swedish (person), Suēden-jin
(to) **sweep**, haku [*hah-koo*] (hakimasu)
sweet, amai [*ah-mah'ee*]
sweetheart, koibito [*koh'ee-bee-toh*]
(to) **swim**, oyogu [*oh-yoh-goo*] (oyogimasu)
sword, katana [*kah-tah-nah*]

table, teburu [*teh-boo-roo*]
tail, o [*oh*]
tailor, shitate ya [*shee-tah-teh yah*]
Taiwan, Taiwan [*Tah'ee-wahn*]
Taiwan (person), Taiwan-jin
(to) **take**, toru [*toh-roo*] (torimasu)
  take it, tori nasai [*toh-ree nah-sah'ee*]
  Take care of it. Kore wo kanri shite kudasai.
    [*Koh-reh woh kahn-ree shee-teh koo-dah-sah'ee.*]
(to) **talk**, hanasu [*hah-nahss*] (hanashimasu)
tall, takai [*tah-kah'ee*]
talent, sainō [*sah'ee-*NOH]
tank, tanku [*tahn-koo*]
tape, tēpu [TEH-*poo*]
tape recorder, tepu rekōdā [TEH-*poo* reh-KOH-
  DAH]
taste, aji [*ah-jee*]
(to) **taste**, ajiwu [*ah-jee-woo*] (ajiwaimasu)
tax, zeikin [*zeh'ee-kin*]
taxi, takushī [*tahk-*SHEE]
tea, ocha [*oh-chah*]
tea ceremony, chanoyu [*chah-noh-yoo*]
(to) **teach**, oshieru [*oh-shee-eh-roo*] (oshiemasu)
teacher, sensei [*sehn-seh'ee*]
teahouse, kissaten [*kees-sah-tehn*], or chaya
  [*chah-yah*]
telegram, denpō [*dehn-*POH]
telephone, denwa [*dehn-wah*]
telephone operator, kōkanshu [KOH-*kahn-shoo*]

television, terebi [*teh-reh-bee*]
(to) tell, iu [*ee-yoo*] (iimasu)
  tell him, kare ni itte kudasai [*kah-reh nee it-teh koo-dah-sah'ee*]
  tell her, kanojo ni itte kudasai [*kah-noh-joh nee it-teh koo-dah-sah'ee*]
  tell me, watakushi ni itte kudasai [*wah-tahk-shee nee it-teh koo-dah-sah'ee*]
temper, kishitsu [*kee-sheet-soo*]
temperature, ondo [*on-doh*]
temple, tera [*teh-rah*]
ten, jū [JOO]
terrace, terasu [*teh-rahss*]
terrible, hidoi [*hee-doh'ee*]
test, shiken [*shee-kehn*]
than, yori [*yoh-ree*]
Thank you! Arigatō! [*Ah-ree-gah-*TOH!]
that, sore [*soh-reh*]
theater, gekijō [*gheh-kee-*JOH]
their (theirs), karera no [*kah-reh-rah noh*]
them, karera wo [*kah-reh-rah woh*]
  to them, karera ni [*kah-reh-rah nee*]
there, asoko [*ah-soh-koh*]
  there is, there are (for things), arimasu [*ah-ree-mahss*]
  there is not (for things), arimasen [*ah-ree-mah-sehn*]
  Is there? (for things), Arimasu ka? [*Ah-ree-mahss kah?*]
  there is, there are (for people and animals), imasu [*ee-mahss*]
  there is not (for people and animals) imasen [*ee-mah-sehn*]
  Is there? (for people and animals), Imasu ka? [*Ee-mahss kah?*]

therefore, desu kara [*dehss kah-rah*]

thermometer, kandankei [*kahn-dahn-keh'ee*]

these, korera no [*koh-reh-rah noh*]

they, karera wa [*kah-reh-rah wah*]

thick, futoi [*foo-toh'ee*]

thief, dorobō [*doh-roh-*BOH]

thin, hosoi [*hoh-soh'ee*]

thing, mono [*moh-noh*]

(to) **think,** omou [*oh-moh'oo*] (omoimasu)

    What do you think about it? Dō omoimasu ka?
    [DOH *oh-moh'ee-mahss kah?*]

third, sambamme no [*sahm-bahm-meh noh*]

(to be) **thirsty,** nodo ga kawaite iru [*noh-doh gah
    kah-wah'ee-teh ee-roo*] (nodo ga kawaite imasu)

thirteen, jūsan [JOO-*sahn*]

thirty, sanjū [*sahn-*JOO]

this, kono [*koh-noh*] Example: "kono hon" **this
    book**

those, sorera [*soh-reh-rah*]

thousand, sen [*sehn*]

thread, ito [*ee-toh*]

three, san [*san*] or mittsu [*meet-tsoo*]

throne, woza [*woh-zah*]

through (finished), owari made [*oh-wah-ree mah-
    deh*]

(to) **throw,** nageru [*nahg-eh-roo*] (nagemasu)

Thursday, Mokuyōbi [*Moh-koo-*YOH-*bee*]

thus (like this), yue ni [*yoo-eh nee*]

ticket, kippu [*kip-poo*]

tiger, tora [*toh-rah*]

tight, katai [*kah-tah'ee*]

time, toki [*toh-kee*]

    At what time? Nan ji ni? [*Nahn jee nee?*]

tin, buriki [*boo-ree-kee*]

tip, kokorozuke [*koh-koh-roh-zoo-keh*]

tired, tsukareta [*tsoo-kah-reh-tah*]

tire (automobile), taiya [*tah'ee-yah*]

to (for people), ni [*nee*] (used *after* noun or pronoun. Example: **to him** "kare ni")

to (for places), e [*eh*] (Example: "Tōkyo e" **to Tokyo**)

toast, tōsuto [TOHS-*toh*]

tobacco, tabako [*tah-bah-koh*]

today, kyō [*k'*YOH]

toe, ashiyubi [*ah-shee-yoo-bee*]

together, to issho ni [*toh ees-shoh nee*]

toilet, kesho shitsu [*keh-shoh sheet-soo*]

toilet paper, chiri gami [*chee-ree gah-mee*]

tomato, tomato [*toh-mah-toh*]

tomb, haka [*hah-kah*]

tongue, shita [*shee-tah*]

tonight, konya [*kohn-yah*]

too, sugiru [*soo-gee-roo*]

tooth, ha [*hah*]

  I have a toothache. ha ga itai [*hah gah ee-tah'ee*]

toothbrush, ha burashu [*hah brahsh*]

top, chōjō [CHOH-JOH]

total, gōkei [GO-*keh'ee*]

(to) touch, sawaru [*sah-wah-roo*] (sawarimasu)

tough, jōbu na [JOH-*boo nah*]

tour, ryokō [*r'yoh*-KOH]

tourist, kanko kyaku [*kahn-koh k'yah-koo*]

towards, no hō e [*noh* HOH *eh*]

towel, tenugui [*tehn-gwee*]

town, machi [*mah-chee*]

toy, omocha [*oh-moh-chah*]

trade, shōgyō [SHOH-*g'*YOH]

traffic, kōtsū [KOHT-SOO]

train, kisha [*kee-shah*]

(to) **transfer,** norikaeru [*noh-ree-kah-eh-roo*] (norikaemasu)

transistor, toranjisutā [*toh-rahn-jee-soo-*TAH]

(in) **transit,** tensōchū [*tehn-*SOH-CHOO]

translation, honyaku [*hohn-yah-koo*]

transportation, yusō [*yoo-*SOH]

(to) **travel,** ryokō suru [*r'yoh-*KOH *soo-roo*] (ryokō shimasu)

tree, ki [*kee*]

trick, hiketsu [*hee-keht-soo*]

trip, ryokō [*r'yoh-*KOH]

  Have a good trip! Dōzo yoi ryokō wo! [DOH-*zoh yoh'ee r'yoh-*KOH *woh!*]

trollycar, densha [*dehn-shah*]

tropical, nettai no [*neht-tah'ee noh*]

trouble, nangi [*nahn-ghee*]

truck, torakku [*toh-rahk-koo*]

true, seitō na [*seh'ee-*TOH *nah*]

truth, shinjitsu [*shin-jeet-soo*]

(to) **try,** tamesu [*tah-meh-soo*] (tameshimasu)

Tuesday, Kayōbi [*Kah-*YOH-*bee*]

tulip, chūrippu [CHOO-*reep-poo*]

tune, fushi [*foo-shee*]

tunnel, chikadō [*chee-kah-*DOH]

typhoon, taifū [*tah'ee-*FOO]

Turkey, Toruko [*Toh-roo-koh*]

Turkish (language), Toruko-go

Turkish (person), Toruko-jin

(to) **turn,** mawaru [*mah-wah-roo*] (mawarimasu)

twelve, jūni [JOO-*nee*]

twenty, nijū [*nee-*JOO]

two, ni [*nee*] or futatsu [*foo-tah-tsoo*]

type (sort), kata [*kah-tah*]

(to) **type** (on typewriter) taipu wo utsu [*tah'ee-poo woh oo-tsoo*] (taipo wo uchimasu)

typewriter, taipuraitā [*tah'eep-rah'ee-*TAH]

typical, dokutoku na [*doh-koo-toh-koo nah*]
typist, taipisuto [*tah'ee-pees-toh*]

ugly, minikui [*mee-nee-koo'ee*]
umbrella, kasa [*kah-sah*]
uncle, oji [*oh-jee*]
uncomfortable, fukai na [*foo-kah'ee nah*]
unconscious, muishiki no [*moo'ee-shee-kee noh*]
under, no shita ni [*noh shee-tah nee*]
(to) understand, wakaru [*wah-kah-roo*] (wakarimasu)
  Do you understand? Wakarimasu ka? [*Wah-kah-ree-mahss kah?*]
underwear, shitagi [*shee-tah-ghee*]
unemployed, shitsugyōshita [*sheet-soo-g'YOH-shee-tah*]
unequal, hitoshiku nai [*hee-toh-shee-koo nah'ee*]
unfair, fukōhei na [*foo-КОН-heh'ee nah*]
unfortunate, fuun na [*foo-oon nah*]
ungrateful, fuyukai na [*foo-yoo-kah'ee nah*]
unhealthy, fukenkō na [*foo-kehn-КОН nah*]
uniform, seifuku [*seh'ee-foo-koo*]
unimportant, jūyō de nai [*JOO-YOH deh nah'ee*]
union, kumiai [*koo-mee-ah'ee*]
United Kingdom, Rengō Ōkoku [*Rehn-GOH OH-koh-koo*]
United States of America, Amerika Gasshūkoku [*Ah-meh-ree-kah Gas-SHOO-koh-koo*]
universal, uchū no [*oo-CHOO noh*]
university, daigaku [*dah'ee-gah-koo*]
unlawful, fuhō no [*foo-HOH noh*]
unlucky, fukō na [*foo-КОН nah*]
(to) unpack, ni wo toku [*nee woh toh-koo*] (ni wo tokimasu)
unpleasant, fuyukai na [*foo-yoo-kah'ee nah*]
unsafe, anzen de nai [*ahn-zehn deh nah'ee*]

until, made [*mah-deh*]
untrue, uso no [*oo-soh noh*]
unusual, mezurashii [*meh-zoo-rah-shee'ee*]
upper, takai hō no [*tah-kah'ee* HOH *noh*]
upstairs, nikai ni [*nee-kah'ee nee*]
urgent, kinkyū no [*kin-k'*YOO *noh*]
us, watakushitachi wo [*wah-tahk-shee-tah-chee woh*]
  (to) **us,** watakushitachi ni [*wah-tahk-shee-tah-chee nee*]
(to) **use,** tsukau [*tsoo-kah'oo*] (tsukaimasu)
useful, yūyō na [YOO-YOH *nah*]
useless, muyō na [*moo-*YOH *nah*]
usual, futsū no [*foot-*soo *noh*]
usually, futsū [*foot-*soo]

vacant, kūkan [KOO-*kahn*]
vacation, kyūka [*k'*YOO-*kah*]
vaccination, yobō chūsha [*yoh-*BOH CHOO-*shah*]
valuable, kōka na [KOH-*kah nah*]
value, neuchi [*neh'oo-chee*]
variety, tashu [*tah-shoo*]
various, shuju no [*shoo-joo noh*]
veal, koushi no niku [*koh'oo-shee noh nee-koo*]
vegetables, yasai [*yah-sah'ee*]
velvet, birōdo [*bee-*ROH-*doh*]
very, hijō ni [*hee-*JOH *nee*]
vest, chokki [*chock-kee*]
view, keshiki [*keh-shee-kee*]
village, mura [*moo-rah*]
vinegar, su [*soo*]
violin, baiorin [*bah'ee-oh-reen*]
(to) **visit,** hōmon suru [HOH-*mon soo-roo*] (hōmon
  shimasu)

voice, koe [*koh'eh*]
volcano, kazan [*kah-zan*]

(to) wait, matsu [*maht-soo*] (machimasu)
waiter, boi [*boy*]
waitress, kyuji [*k'yoo-jee*]
waiting room, machiaishitsu [*mah-chee'ah'ee-sheet-soo*]
(to) wake up, me ga sameru [*meh gah sah-meh-roo*] (me ga samemasu)
(to) walk, aruku [*ah-roo-koo*] (arukimasu)
  (to) take a walk, sanpo suru [*san-poh soo-roo*] (sanpo shimasu)
wallet, saifu [*sah'ee-foo*]
wall, kabe [*kah-beh*]
(to) want,

> NOTE: To express **to want** with the object wanted, use "hoshii desu" preceded by "ga." Example: "Matchi ga hoshii desu." **I want a match.** To express **to want to do something** use "tai" and "desu" with the polite stem of the verb like this: "Ikitai desu." **I want to go.** "Ikitaku arimasen." **I do not want to go.**

war, sensō [*sehn-*SOH]
warm, atatakai [*ah-tah-tah-kah'ee*]
(to) wash, arau [*ah-rah'oo*] (araimasu)
(to) waste, muda ni suru [*moo-dah nee soo-roo*] (muda ni shimasu)
watch or **clock,** tokei [*toh-keh'ee*]
(to) watch, miru [*mee-roo*] (mimasu)
water, mizu [*mee-zoo*]
water (hot), oyu [*oh-yoo*]
waterfall, taki [*tah-kee*]
wave, nami [*nah-mee*]

way (to destination), hōkō [:IOH-KOH]

way (manner), hōhō [HOH-HOH]

   By the way... Sorewasote [Soh-reh-wah-SOH-teh]

weak, yowai [yoh-wah'ee]

(to) **wear** (coats, shirts, etc.), kiru [kee-roo] (kimasu)

(to) **wear** (pants), haku [hah-koo] (hakimasu)

weather, tenki [tehn-kee]

wedding, kekkon [kehk-kohn]

(to) **weigh** or **measure,** hakaru [hah-kah-roo] (hakarimasu)

(to) **welcome,** kangei sareru [kahn-geh'ee sah-reh-roo] (kangei saremasu)

(you are) **welcome,** do itashimashite [doh ee-tah-shee-mah-shee-teh]

we, watakushitachi [wah-tahk-shee-tah-chee]

west, nishi [nee-shee]

wet, nureta [noo-reh-tah]

   (to) **get wet,** nureru [noo-reh-roo] (nuremasu)

whale, kujira [koo-jee-rah]

what, nani [nah-nee]

   What else? Hoka ni? [Hoh-kah nee?]

   What of it? Kamai masen? [Kah-mah'ee mah-sehn?]

wheel, kuruma [kuh-ruh-mah] (also used as "automobile")

when, itsu [it-soo]

where, doko [doh-koh]

   Where to? Doko e? [Doh-koh eh?]

   Where is it? Doko desu ka? [Doh-koh dehss kah!]

which, dochira [doh-chee-rah]

while, aida [ah'ee-dah]

white, shiro [shee-roh]

who, dare [dah-reh]

Who is it? Dare desu ka? [*Dah-reh dehss kah?*]
whole, zentai [*zehn-tah'ee*]
whom, dare wo [*dah-reh woh*]
  to whom? dare ni? [*dah-reh nee?*]
whose, dare no [*dah-reh noh*]
wife (mine), tsuma [*tsoo-mah*]
  (yours), okusan [*ohk-sahn*]
wild, yasei [*yah-seh'ee*]
will,

> NOTE: The future tense is expressed by adding
> "masho" to the polite stem or "desho" to the
> infinitive. This indicates the *probable* future.
> **I write.** "Kakimasu." **I will** (probably) **write.**
> "Kakimasho." (or) "Kaku desho."

willow, yanagi [*yah-nah-ghee*]
(to) win, katsu [*kaht-soo*] (kachimasu)
wind, kaze [*kah-zeh*]
window, mado [*mah-doh*]
wine, budō shu [*boo-DOH shoo*]
wing, hane [*hah-neh*]
winter, fuyu [*foo-yoo*]
wire, harigane [*hah-ree-gah-neh*]
wise, rikō [*ree-KOH*]
(to) wish, see (to) want
with, to [*toh*]
without, nashi ni [*nah-shee nee*]
wolf, ōkami [*OH-kah-mee*]
woman, onna [*ohn-nah*]
wonderful, subarashii [*soo-bah-rah-shee'ee*]
wood, ki [*kee*]
woods, hayashi [*hah-yah-shee*]
wool, yōmō [*YOH-MOH*]
word, kotaba [*koh-tah-bah*]
(to) work, hataraku [*hah-tah-rah-koo*] (hataraki-
    masu)

world, sekai [*seh-kah'ee*]
(to) **worry,** shinpai suru [*shin-pah'ee soo-roo*]
(shinpai shimasu)
Don't worry! Shinpai shinai de! [*Sheen-pah'ee shee-nah'ee deh!*]
worse, motto warui [*moht-toh wah-roo'ee*]
(I) would like to ......
would you like to ......?

NOTE: Simply use the polite form of any verb.
Example: "Ikimasu." **I would like to go.**
Add the question "ka" after any polite form. Example: "Ikimasu ka?" **Would you (he, she, they), like to go?**

wrist, tekubi [*teh-koo-bee*]
(to) **write,** kaku [*kah-koo*] (kakimasu)
wrong, machigai [*mah-chee-gah'ee*]

yacht, yotto [*yoht-toh*]
year, nen [*nehn*]
last year, sakunen [*sah-koo-nehn*]
next year, rainen [*rah'ee-nehn*]
yellow, kiiro [*kee'ee-roh*]
yes, hai [*hah'ee*]
yesterday, sakujitsu [*sah-koo-jit-soo*]
not yet, mada desu [*mah-dah dehss*]
you, anata [*ah-nah-tah*]
young, wakai [*wah-kah'ee*]
your, yours, anata no [*ah-nah-tah noh*]

zero, rei [*reh'ee*]
zipper, chakku [*chah-koo*]
zoo, dōbutsu en [DOH-*boo-tsoo ehn*]

YOU KNEW MORE THAN 1000 WORDS OF JAPANESE BEFORE YOU STARTED THIS BOOK!

How is it possible? Due to Japan's modernization and increasing commercial ties to the West, many English words have been adopted wholesale into Japanese, with some pronunciation changes and occasional simplifications. Here are some examples of English words which have crossed the Pacific and made a new home in the "Rising Sun" country. They are arranged according to categories. You will recognize most of them, but just to make sure, we have added the meaning of each after the Japanese spelling in Roma-ji (the Japanese word for Japanese when written in Roman letters).

FOOD & DRINK

raisu – rice   **bata** – butter   **suteiki** – steak
rōsuto bifu – roast beef   **bēkon** – bacon   **sarada** – salad   **omuretsu** – omelette   **keiku** – cake
meron – melon   **remon** – lemon   **shokoreto** – chocolate   **aisukurimū** – ice cream   **sosu** – sauce   **kyandē** – candy   **supū** – soup   **chizu** – cheese   **desato** – dessert   **tosuto** – toast
tomato – tomato   **paseri** – parsley   **mayonezu** – mayonnaise   **pai** – pie   **retasu** – lettuce
gureipu furūtsu – grapefruit   **furai** – fried
sosejī – sausage   **sandoichi** – sandwich   **sodā** – soda   **sheri** – sherry   **arukorū** – alcohol
remonēdo – lemonade   **koka kora** – coca cola
sanpen – champagne   **wain** – wine   **bīru** – beer
miruku – milk   **oranji jusu** – orange juice
uisukī – whisky   **kohee** – coffee   **burandī** – brandy   **jin** – gin

NIGHT LIFE

restoran – restaurant   **guriru** – grill   **kyabare** – cabaret   **kafuē** – café (sidewalk)   **fuirumu** – film   **ōkestora** – orchestra (western)   **bando** – band   **menyū** – menu   **dansu** – to dance   **kurabu** – club   **hosutesu** – hostess   **naito kurabu** – night club   **kabā chaji** – cover charge   **shō** – show   **furewa sho** – floor show

DRUGS, COSMETICS & TOBACCO

asupurin – aspirin   **kōrudo kurīmu** – cold cream   **matchi** – match   **tabako** – tobacco   **shigaretto** – cigarette   **sumoku** – to smoke   **paipu** – pipe   **chūin gamu** – chewing gum   **heyā tonikku** – hair tonic

CLOTHING & MAINTENANCE

sūtsu – suit   **botan** – button   **pantee** – panties   **doresu** – dress   **sueta** – sweater   **hankachi** – handkerchief   **handobaggu** – handbag   **sukāfu** – scarf   **nekutai** – necktie   **obakoto** – overcoat   **sutokingu** – stocking   **waishatsu** – (white) shirt   **burausu** – blouse   **sukāto** – skirt   **poketto** – pocket   **setto** – set (hair)   **pamanento** – permanent   **manikuya** – manicure

AROUND THE HOUSE

apāto – apartment   **erebeta** – elevator   **hoteru** – hotel   **birudingu** – building   **puru** – pool   **barukoni** – balcony   **terasu** – terrace   **rampu** – lamp   **teburu** – table   **stobu** – stove   **ragu** – rug   **garasu** – glass   **kāten** – curtain   **supunu** – spoon   **naifu** – knife   **fuoku** – fork   **napukin** – napkin   **taoru** – towel   **kan** – can (tin can)   **shawa** – shower   **rekodo** – record

kamera – camera   **pin** – pin   **tepu rekodā** –
tape recorder   **rekodō pureyā** – record player
terebi – television   **inku** – ink   **toranjisutā** –
transistor   **airon** – iron (pressing)   **sutureo** –
stereo   **rajio** – radio   **niusu** – the news

CARS

ka – car   **motosaiku** – motorcycle   **basu** – bus
torakku – truck   **takushi** – taxi   **garaji** –
garage   **gasorin** – gasoline   **garon** – gallon
tanku – tank   **fan beruto** – fan belt   **oiru** – oil
batteri – battery   **motā** – motor   **fendā** –
fender   **taiya** – tire   **puragu** – plug   **noku** –
knock   **kaburetā** – carburetor   **giya** – gear

SPORTS

supotsu – sports   **metaru** – medal   **supiido** –
speed   **gorufu** – golf   **suki** – ski   **suketo** –
skate   **yotto** – yachting   **hokki** – hockey
tenisu – tennis   **hoomurun** – home run
sutoraiku – strike   **basukettoboru** – basketball
boru – ball   **aūtō!** – out!   **seifu!** – safe!

BUSINESS

kosto – cost   **meka** – maker, manufacturer
sararimanu – salaried man   **seru** – sale   **ado** –
advertising   **depato** – department store
rāshawa – rush hour   **supamaketo** – supermarket
saresmanu – salesman   **sābisu** – service
taipisuto – typist   **taipuraitā** – typewriter
surogan – slogan   **moderu** – model

ATTENTION!

Before going abroad you may want to take a few lessons or a complete course in your favorite language at one of the many Berlitz Schools of Languages in North America. Among the following you will surely find one near you:

AKRON, Ohio	NEW YORK, New York
ATLANTA, Georgia	OAKLAND, California
BALTIMORE, Maryland	ORANGE, California
BEVERLY HILLS, California	OTTAWA, Ont., Canada
BIRMINGHAM, Michigan	PALO ALTO, California
BOSTON, Massachusetts	PASADENA, California
CALGARY, Alta., Canada	PHILADELPHIA, Pennsylvania
CEDARHURST, New York	PHOENIX, Arizona
CHICAGO, Illinois	PITTSBURGH, Pennsylvania
CINCINNATI, Ohio	PONCE, Puerto Rico
CLEVELAND, Ohio	PROVIDENCE, Rhode Island
DALLAS, Texas	QUEBEC, P. Q., Canada
DENVER, Colorado	RIDGEWOOD, New Jersey
DETROIT, Michigan	ST. HYACINTHE, P. Q., Canada
EAST ORANGE, New Jersey	ST. LOUIS, Missouri
EDMONTON, Alta., Canada	SAN DIEGO, California
FOREST HILLS, New York	SAN FRANCISCO, California
FORT WORTH, Texas	SAN JUAN, Puerto Rico
GUADALAJARA, Mexico	SEATTLE, Washington
HOUSTON, Texas	SHERBROOKE, P. Q., Canada
JOLIETTE, P. Q., Canada	SHERMAN OAKS, California
LOS ANGELES, California	STAMFORD, Connecticut
MANHASSET, New York	TORONTO, Ont., Canada
MEXICO CITY, Mexico	TROIS RIVIERES, P. Q., Canada
MIAMI, Florida	VANCOUVER, B. C., Canada
MILWAUKEE, Wisconsin	WASHINGTON, D. C.
MINNEAPOLIS, Minnesota	WHITE PLAINS, New York
MONTREAL, P. Q., Canada	WINNETKA, Illinois

Elsewhere in the world you may wish to take some lessons at the Berlitz schools in the following major cities: Paris, London, Rome, Trieste, Munich, Vienna, Madrid, Barcelona, Johannesburg, Rio de Janeiro, Buenos Aires, Helsinki, Casablanca, Istanbul or Tokyo.

BUSINESS REPLY CARD

First Class Permit No. 13017, Sec. 34.9, P. L. & R., New York, N. Y.

CENTRAL EXECUTIVE OFFICES
THE BERLITZ SCHOOLS OF LANGUAGES
866 THIRD AVENUE
NEW YORK, NEW YORK 10022

Gentlemen:

☐ I am interested in studying _____

☐ I should like to attend school in _____
   (language)

☐ I should like to know about self-instruction books.
   (city)

☐ I should like information about the Berlitz Self-Teaching Record Courses.

Please advise me, without obligation.

401

Name _____

Street _____

City and State _____

Telephone No. _____